BOB- :KAUFFMANN

CONSOLIDATION OF THE VOID

The Architecture of Deception and the Reclamation of Agency

The Sovereign Patent & Reservation of Rights

This physical volume and its contents operate as a bridging mechanism between the material distribution network and the higher frequency of the Chief Cornerstone. The author, Robert-John: [Kauffmann], retains sole, unalienable authorship and complete ownership of all intellectual property, raw data, drafts, and concepts contained herein. The purchase, possession, or distribution of this physical book does not constitute a forfeiture of the author's inherent sovereignty, nor does it establish an adhesion contract, joinder, or trust with any administrative, corporate, or maritime jurisdiction.

Typographical & Semantic Notice

Within this text, the utilization of capitalized nomenclature (e.g., ALL-CAPS) is deployed strictly for emphasis, structural clarity, or the forensic identification of systemic Dog-Latin. Under no circumstances does the use of capitalized terms within this volume constitute a recognition of, or joinder to, a dead corporate fiction (The Strawman). All names and titles are utilized without prejudice to the standing of the biological Living Man.

Disclaimer of Liability & Standing

The forensic analysis, legal writs, and spiritual protocols contained within The Consolidation of the Void are provided strictly for the purpose of profound educational inquiry and the Reclamation of Agency. This work does not constitute licensed legal, financial, medical, or psychological advice. True sovereignty requires the absolute assumption of personal liability; the author holds no joinder, contract, or liability for the physical, legal, or frequency outcomes experienced by the reader in the application of these protocols. The reader acknowledges that they are a self-governing entity responsible for their own due diligence.

Forensic Record Notice

This volume is entered into the public record as a Sovereign Witness of the Jurisdictional Void. It is a private communication intended for the Remnant. Any unauthorized "Retroactive Content Injection" or digital overwriting of this work by silicon-based "World Models" is a violation of the author's original Source Code and universal standing.

All rights reserved. Without prejudice.

UCC 1-308 | UCC 1-103.6

First edition

ISBN: 979-8-9955821-0-6

Contents

Foreword

Every age produces its own architecture of power, and with it, a vocabulary designed to make that power invisible. This book, *Consolidation of the Void*, is written for those who have begun to sense the glaring discrepancies between the official narratives of our time and the geopolitical realities unfolding on the ground.

In previous explorations of sovereignty and systemic history, overarching theoretical frameworks may have occasionally overshadowed the immediate, practical actions required of the reader. Theory is no longer sufficient. The intent of this project is not merely to describe a system from afar, but to challenge you to do the necessary work of inquiry—to recognize the walls of a prison you may not know you are financing. This book brings the mechanical elements of your subjugation into sharp, actionable focus.

Today, we find ourselves in an era where the language of diplomacy and humanitarianism is deployed as a weaponized shield. We are told by official bulletins that we are funding a "Decisive Victory for Freedom," yet the underlying data reveals a meticulously managed transition into permanent Administrative Servitude. When the concept of "Peace" is used to market the privatization of statecraft, when international reconstruction boards share the same ledgers as private equity firms, and when the bypass of constitutional checks is framed as a sudden "emergency," the public is left blind to the sheer scale of the extraction taking place.

But the financial cost is merely the machinery of a much deeper theft. They are not just siphoning your national treasury and diluting your purchasing power; they are attempting to harvest your consent and overwrite your spiritual agency. By using sacred mantles to mask a profane, material agenda, the Architects of this system seek to sever the individual from their divine inheritance, replacing the sovereign soul with a managed, trackable asset.

The purpose of this work is to shatter that cognitive seal. It challenges you to look past the philanthropic veneer and examine the cold mechanics of digital consensus, the privatization of global military authority, and the wealth transfers operating in plain sight. More importantly, it is a call to Divine Discernment.

To reclaim one's agency, one must first recognize exactly how, where, and by whom it is being consolidated. The ultimate battle is not fought solely in the ledgers, but in the soul. This book is an imperative to ask the difficult questions, secure your spiritual and material baseline, and step permanently out of the void.

Preface

The Tri-Lateral Engine: Consolidation of the Void

Primary Mechanism: The replacement of national sovereignty with a managed "Void" governed by the Abraham Accords framework.

I. The Tri-Lateral Base (The Engine)

The system is powered by a synchronized objective shared by three distinct poles:

- **The United States:** Providing the legal and military umbrella (CENTCOM integration) to shield the transition.
- **The State of Israel:** Acting as the technological and "Startup Nation" hub, injecting advanced surveillance and defense systems into the architecture.
- **The Sunni Gulf Monarchies:** Serving as the capital engine, utilizing sovereign wealth funds to finance the infrastructure of the new jurisdiction.

II. The Connective Tissue (Private Equity & Dual-Purpose Envoys)

The true "gears" of this engine are not traditional diplomats, but **Dual-Purpose Negotiators**.

- **The Ledger:** These individuals operate simultaneously as State Envoys and Directors of Private Equity Firms.
- **The Friction:** By managing both the military aid (state side) and the infrastructure investment (private side), they create a state of **Permanent Economic and Military Friction**. This friction is necessary to justify the continued "management" of the Void and the extraction of value from

regional resources.

III. The Theological Veneer (The Shield)

The entire architecture is wrapped in an interfaith, "Abrahamic" narrative.

- **The Function:** This veneer serves to shield the **Dual-Purpose Ledgers** from the light of truth. By framing a corporate and military realignment as a "spiritual homecoming" or "interfaith peace," the Architects prevent the "profane" from questioning the underlying dismantling of their own national and individual sovereignty.

IV. The Mandatory Disclosure (The Requirement of Justice)

Justice requires the **Total Disclosure** of these ledgers. The unmasking of the "Privateer" influence within the Abraham Accords is the only way to dissolve the Void and restore the light of Truth to the children of Abraham.

Introduction

In the current global landscape, the public exists within a carefully curated mirage. If one relies solely on the digital feeds, official state bulletins, and the consensus of the captured representative class, the world appears chaotic but ultimately managed by well-meaning institutions striving for peace. We are told that kinetic operations—like the devastating escalations of Epic Fury— are unfortunate but necessary steps toward a "Decisive Victory for Freedom."

The underlying material data, however, reveals a chilling inverse reality.

We are not witnessing the defense of the constitutional republic; we are witnessing its controlled demolition. The chaos is not accidental; it is engineered. The resulting geopolitical shifts are not leading to human liberation, but to a meticulously managed transition into permanent Administrative Servitude.

At the center of this transition is a concept we must accurately define: **The Void**.

The Void is not an empty space. It is a deliberate, highly structured jurisdictional and legal vacuum created by trans-national elites. It is the space where the War Powers Act goes dormant, where international law is overwritten by privateer contracts, and where national sovereignty, individual agency, and private wealth are silently siphoned into a trans-national shadow architecture. To operate within the Void is to operate with absolute impunity, immune to the audits of the public and the checks of a constitutional republic.

To understand how the Architects of the Void maintain this illusion while executing the greatest wealth transfer in human history, we must deconstruct the foundation of their machine. The entire system of deception rests upon three structural pillars:

PILLAR I: The Mirage of Consensus

To drain the treasury of a republic in broad daylight, the system requires a mandate. Because a genuine grassroots mandate for endless conflict and the hollowing out of the middle class does not exist, it must be manufactured.

Contemporary narratives claim a "monolith of support" for escalating regional strikes and global interventionism. This is a Statistical Mirage. By utilizing AI-driven "Silicon Guards"—deploying biohybrid swarms for physical surveillance and algorithmic saturation for digital control—the Architects filter out organic dissent. Through the weaponization of "World Models" and Retroactive Content Injection, the system actively overwrites the digital archive to create a false consensus. This mechanism intentionally isolates the individual, preventing them from recognizing the significant 56% majority that actually opposes the current escalations. You are not outnumbered; you are simply being out-broadcast by a False Vanguard.

PILLAR II: The Privateer State & The Economic Engine

The modern era of warfare is no longer driven by the clash of sovereign nation-states; it is driven by the profit motives of the Privateer State.

Entities like the Board of Peace (BoP) are aggressively marketed to the public as humanitarian responses to regional crises. However, their internal charters reveal a permanent, global mandate for acquisition. Under this pillar, war is reclassified as a zoning opportunity. The "Gaza-First" prototype serves as the ultimate beta test for Disaster Capitalism on Steroids. By utilizing military forces as a taxpayer-funded demolition crew, the Architects clear sovereign land to build "Workforce Housing" and exclusive trans-national economic zones like the Eastern Mediterranean Riviera. They utilize biometric controls, Chapter VII legal silences, and programmable debt to create a scalable model for regional expansion into any "hotspot."

This is fueled by a massive extraction of public wealth: a $200 Billion Siphon of national liquidity, facilitated by legislative bypasses and central bank monetization, while the physical hardware is funded through the $5 Billion Parallel and directed by unaccountable private equity envoys.

PILLAR III: The Theological Shield & Spiritual Fraud

This is the most sophisticated and impenetrable layer of the architecture, for it bridges the gap between the material and the spiritual. The Architects know that raw, financial extraction is optically toxic. Therefore, they wrap their secular operations in a protected religious and ethnic mantle.

This is the ultimate spiritual fraud: the deception of those who claim a sacred identity to run a profane, material agenda. In biblical terms, this assembly of adversaries operates as the Synagogue of Satan. By using sacred mantles to justify kinetic slaughter, the principals have created a Jurisdictional Shield. They trigger a "Cognitive Seal" in the public mind—a programmed reflexive dismissal that instantly labels any investigation into their $157 Million fee ledgers or diplomatic sabotage as "hateful" or "extremist." This programmed blindness allows the occult engine to extract both capital and human life force (*loosh*) uninterrupted behind a veneer of untouchable sanctity.

The Map Out of the Machine

You cannot defeat an architecture of power until you can clearly see its blueprints.

The chapters that follow will systematically dismantle these three pillars. We will audit the Shadow Architecture, tracking the capital from the Omnibus Extortion to the $157M Affinity ledgers. We will map the "Kinetic Subcontract" that turns our youth into mercenaries for private equity. We will dissect the Jurisdictional Void and the Scapegoat Protocols designed to trap the public in perpetual security fees.

Finally, through the Sovereign Documentation provided in the Appendices, we will provide the receipts: the fee ledgers, the conflict maps, and the structural discrepancies in the BoP Charters.

Most importantly, we will establish the "Sovereign Baseline"—the spiritual and material foundation required to starve the machine of your consent. Through asset hardening, the establishment of a parallel economy, and the assertion of the Living Man's jurisdiction, we will outline the mechanics of a functional exit.

The mirage is breaking. It is time to look at the ledger.

The 1933-2026 Transition: The Wizard's Final Act

The *Wizard of Oz* was released in 1939, but its "Mechanical Audit" is rooted in the events of 1933—the year the Republic was moved into a permanent **Jurisdictional Void**. To understand the 2026 transition to a digital panopticon, one must understand the first transition from **Substance** to **Shadow**.

1. The 1933 Confiscation (The Yellow Brick Road is Closed)

In 1933, under **Executive Order 6102**, the "Substance" (Gold) was confiscated from the people. The "Yellow Brick Road"—the path back to real value and individual sovereignty—was effectively closed.

- **The Veneer:** The public was told this was a temporary necessity for "Economic Stabilization" during a manufactured crisis.
- **The Hardware:** This was the birth of the **Straw Man**. When the gold was removed, the **Living Man** could no longer pay his debts *at law* (which requires a transfer of substance). Instead, he was forced to "discharge" them in equity using the Wizard's paper notes. This turned every American into a **Tin Man**—a hollowed-out corporate vessel working for a heartless administrative grid, lacking the "heart" of true ownership.

2. The Archetypes of the Enclosure

The Wizard's machine relies on three specific human failures to maintain the Void:

- **The Scarecrow:** Represents the uninitiated whose thoughts are "stuffed with straw." He suffers from **Reflexive Dismissal**, unable to process the forensic audit because his perception is managed by the Wizard's curriculum.

- **The Tin Man:** The hollowed-out corporate entity. He has no heart because he has no substance; he is merely a "User" of the Wizard's assets, a biological gear in the **Privateer State**.
- **The Cowardly Lion:** Represents the **Sovereign** who has the inherent power of the **Chief Cornerstone** but has been conditioned by **Systemic Agoraphobia**. He possesses the authority to roar, yet he trembles before the Wizard's projection.

3. The 2026 Shift (The Digital Curtain)

Just as 1933 removed the gold, the current 2026 architecture—led by the **Board of Peace** and **Resolution 2803**—is designed to remove the paper. This is the "Final Consolidation."

- **The Invisible Confiscation:** By moving off paper and into programmable **Central Bank Digital Currencies (CBDCs)**, the Wizard no longer needs to send agents to your door to seize your assets. He simply "reprograms" the ledger. Your wealth is no longer your property; it is a conditional "Digital Credit" subject to a **User Agreement**.
- **The Digital Tether:** In 1933, they took the gold. In 2026, they are taking the **Agency**. If your "Digital Straw Man" does not comply with the administrative mandates of the **Shadow Architecture**, your ability to "buy or sell" is toggled off at the source. This is the mechanical reality of the **Biometric Tether**.

4. The Emerald Glasses vs. The Biometric Lens

In the 1930s, the "Emerald Glasses" were the propaganda of the New Deal, forcing everyone to see a "Green" recovery that was actually a debt-trap. Today, the glasses have been replaced by the **Biometric Lens**.

The Wizard is once again hiding behind a "Crisis" (The Regional Reconstruction/Epic Fury) to justify a final enclosure. They are moving the **Living Man** into a digital **Void** where the individual has no standing, only a "Digital Profile" that can be edited, censored, or deleted.

5. Pulling Back the Curtain

The message of 1933 was that the Wizard has no power unless you believe in his paper. The message of 2026 is that the Wizard has no power unless you accept his digital tether.

Dorothy's **Silver Slippers** (changed to Ruby for the 1939 film to showcase Technicolor) represented the **Power of Silver**—the ability of the individual to walk on their own substance. The transition from Paper to Digital is the attempt to make the **Straw Man** permanent and the **Sovereign Man** obsolete.

The Final Audit: You have always had the power to return "Home"—to the pre-existing jurisdiction of the **Chief Cornerstone**. This book is the manual for clicking your heels and reclaiming your standing.

1

CHAPTER I: THE ANATOMY OF DECEPTIVE CONSENSUS

1.1 The "MAGA" Monolith Myth: Deconstructing Manufactured Support Narratives vs. the Grassroots Reality

To understand how a nation's wealth and agency can be siphoned in broad daylight, one must first understand how its consent is manufactured. In the era of the trans-national shadow architecture, kinetic operations like Epic Fury are not launched against the will of the people—they are launched by completely overriding it, while projecting an illusion of absolute unity.

At the core of this psychological operation is the **"MAGA" Monolith Myth**.

For the architects of the Board of Peace (BoP) and the privateer state to operate with impunity, they require a public mandate. Because a genuine mandate for endless conflict and the draining of national liquidity does not exist, it must be simulated.

The Statistical Mirage: 94% vs. The Grassroots Reality

The modern geopolitical landscape is dominated by a pervasive, top-down narrative asserting that the populist, conservative base—often broadly categorized under the "MAGA" or "America First" umbrella—marches in lockstep with the current administration's foreign policy escalations. Official bulletins, state-aligned media networks, and think-tank polling consistently project a "monolith of support," frequently citing figures as high as 94% unified backing for regional strikes and the expansion of the Abraham Realignment into military hardware.

This is a Statistical Mirage, engineered to paralyze political opposition and gaslight the individual citizen.

When we deconstruct the polling methodologies, strip away the algorithmic amplification, and look at the raw, unweighted grassroots data, a radically different picture emerges:

- **The 56% Majority:** The underlying reality is that a clear 56% majority of the broader electorate actively opposes the kinetic expansion of current conflicts, recognizing them as a drain on domestic stability.
- **The 24% Hard-Core Base:** Within the populist movement itself, only about 24% represents the hard-core, ideologically committed faction that reflexively supports executive military action.

The remaining populace is caught in the "Fog of War," coerced into silence by the engineered perception that they are isolated outliers in a sea of patriotic consensus. By artificially inflating the 24% to look like 94%, the system effectively neutralizes the 56% majority.

The Men Behind the Curtain: Proxies and Privateers

Who benefits from this mirage, and how do they remain hidden? The architects of this deception are rarely the politicians standing at the podium. They are the private equity principals, sovereign wealth managers, and unelected envoys operating in the "Void" between public office and private enterprise—figures like those managing the $157M Affinity Partners ledgers or holding exclusive seats on the Board of Peace.

These influencers hide their material agendas by using the populist base as a human shield. They conceal themselves through three primary mechanisms of laundering:

- **The Think-Tank Astroturf:** By funding "America First" policy institutes and super PACs, private equity billionaires purchase the academic and political vocabulary needed to justify the $200B Siphon. They pay for the white papers that turn a private real estate grab into a "national security imperative."

- **The Unelected Envoy:** The key players avoid Senate confirmation or public accountability by operating as "Special Representatives" or "Senior Advisors." Because they are technically private citizens or sit on international reconstruction boards, their communications and financial entanglements are shielded from standard Freedom of Information Act (FOIA) requests and constitutional oversight.
- **The Influencer Cartel:** They capture the digital public square by financially capturing its loudest voices. By selectively funding independent media networks and digital influencers who already possess high credibility within the MAGA base, they ensure that the "monolith" narrative is delivered by trusted, seemingly grassroots messengers.

The Capture of the Base: Inverting Core Principles

Through these hidden mechanisms, the most insidious aspect of the Monolith Myth is achieved: the weaponization of the sovereignty movement against itself. The grassroots base was fundamentally organized around principles of non-intervention, secure borders, and the dismantling of the bloated administrative state—summed up in the ethos of "No New Wars."

Through the inversion of core principles, the defense of foreign borders is rebranded as an extension of domestic security. The funding of the "Gaza-First" prototype and the privatization of global diplomacy are sold not as nation-building, but as "America First" peacemaking. The grassroots base is continuously fed the rhetoric of sovereignty while the material reality of their nation is systematically hollowed out by the very privateers hiding behind the curtain.

The Function of the Myth

The "MAGA" Monolith Myth serves a singular, vital function for the Consolidation of the Void: Compliance through Isolation. If an individual believes that 94% of their peers support the current kinetic escalations, they are far less likely to voice dissent, question the suspension of constitutional oversight, or investigate the privateer ledgers.

However, a mirage of this magnitude cannot be sustained by traditional media and paid influencers alone. To maintain the illusion of the Monolith, and to actively overwrite the original "No New Wars" mandate, the Architects require a technological enforcement mechanism capable of saturating the digital square and filtering out the 56% majority in real-time.

1.2 Silicon Guard Suppression: Biohybrid Swarms, World Models, and the Death of the Archive

The "MAGA" Monolith Myth cannot sustain itself organically. To maintain the illusion of a 94% consensus while executing the $200B Siphon, the Architects of the Void require a mechanism of enforcement that operates below the threshold of public awareness. They require a system that does not merely censor dissent, but actively overwrites reality.

This enforcement mechanism is the **Silicon Guard**.

Far from the rudimentary algorithms of the early 2020s, the Silicon Guard is a synchronized, multi-domain suppression architecture. It operates across physical, predictive, and historical vectors to ensure that the 56% majority opposing the kinetic escalations of the Board of Peace never realizes its own strength.

The Physical Vector: Biohybrid Swarms

Suppression begins with total physical and acoustic mapping. Traditional digital surveillance is limited by screens and electronic devices; the Silicon Guard bridges this gap using biohybrid technology.

By hijacking the neural pathways of specific biological chassis—most notably, the Madagascar hissing cockroach—engineers have created miniaturized, undetectable sensor nodes. These biohybrid swarms are equipped with micro-acoustic arrays and mesh-networking transmitters. They are deployed into urban centers, political organizing spaces, and areas of high grassroots density to monitor off-grid conversations.

This isn't science fiction; it is the deployed reality of the trans-national shadow state. These swarms provide the real-time, granular acoustic data required to identify nodes of organic dissent before they can coalesce into organized political resistance against the privateer ledgers.

The Predictive Vector: The $1.03B "World Models" (AMI Labs)

Data collection is only the first step; the true power of the Silicon Guard lies in its predictive capacity. Recently, an opaque syndicate of private equity and defense contractors quietly injected $1.03 Billion in seed funding into a new class of artificial intelligence known as "World Models," specifically driven by entities like AMI Labs.

Unlike standard language models that simply generate text, World Models simulate human societies. They map the psychological pressure points of the grassroots base. By feeding the acoustic data from the biohybrid swarms and the digital footprints of the electorate into these models, the Architects can run millions of simulated scenarios per second.

They use these simulations to determine the precise algorithmic saturation required to pacify the public. The World Model calculates exactly how many bot-driven "Cyborg" accounts are needed, what specific "America First" rhetoric must be deployed, and which organic voices must be shadow-filtered to artificially manufacture the 94% consensus. It is a machine designed to automate compliance.

The Historical Vector: Retroactive Content Injection

The most devastating weapon of the Silicon Guard is its ability to alter the past. If a politician campaigned heavily on a "No New Wars" platform, that historical record stands in direct opposition to the current realities of Operation Epic Fury and the suspension of the War Powers Act.

To resolve this contradiction, the Silicon Guard utilizes Retroactive Content Injection.

The era of the static digital archive is dead. Through advanced deep-learning and real-time database manipulation, the system actively overwrites past digital content. An article from three years ago, a video of a campaign speech, or a historical stance on the War Powers Act is subtly, seamlessly altered. The anti-war candidate of the past is retroactively edited to appear as a pragmatic hawk who always supported the concept of "Emergency Stability Operations."

- **The Eradication of Hypocrisy:** Because the past is continuously aligned with the present, the public is denied the evidence of betrayal.
- **The Gaslighting Engine:** When a citizen remembers a promise that no longer exists in the digital record, they do not blame the system; they doubt their own memory.

Through Retroactive Content Injection, the Silicon Guard ensures that the historical ledger always supports the current actions of the Board of Peace. The "Void" is protected not just by hiding the truth of the present, but by erasing the truth of the past.

1.3 Revelation of the Method: The Captured Class and the Management of the "People Farm"

When confronted with the sheer scale of the Board of Peace's global mandate, the $200B liquidity siphon, and the suspension of the War Powers Act, the natural question arises: How has this been allowed to happen by our elected representatives? Where are the constitutional checks and balances?

The brutal reality of the "Void" is that the constitutional republic has been hollowed out. What remains is not a government of, by, and for the people, but an administrative husbandry operation. The nation has been transitioned into a "people farm," where citizens are managed as livestock—taxed, inflated, and algorithmically pacified to produce the liquidity required by the privateer state.

The supposed representatives of the people are no longer public servants; they are the captured managers of this farm.

The Anatomy of Political Capture

The silence of the legislative branch is not an accident; it is engineered. The representative class has been neutralized through a combination of four distinct mechanisms:

- **The Financial Bribe (The Revolving Door):** True bribery in the 2020s is rarely a briefcase of cash. It is the promise of a highly compensated board seat at a private equity firm, a lucrative consulting contract with a defense contractor, or a "humanitarian" appointment within the orbit of the Board of Peace upon leaving office.

- **The Blackmail Ledger:** As detailed in the capabilities of the Silicon Guard, the trans-national intelligence apparatus possesses total digital mapping. Dissenting representatives are quietly reminded of their vulnerabilities—financial, personal, or optical—ensuring their compliance when a "unanimous" vote is required to fund the latest kinetic escalation.
- **Compartmentalization (Willful Ignorance):** Many representatives are simply kept in the dark. By utilizing the "Emergency Stability" loopholes, the Architects bypass congressional oversight entirely. Politicians willingly accept this ignorance, as it provides them with plausible deniability when their constituents eventually ask where the money went.
- **The Uniparty Consensus:** The ultimate capture is ideological. Behind closed doors, the distinction between opposing political parties vanishes when privateer profits and regional "reconstruction" bonds are on the table.

Revelation of the Method: The Psychological Lubricant

To keep the "people farm" docile while its wealth is extracted, these captured managers must employ a sophisticated psychological tool known as Revelation of the Method.

They cannot simply ignore the populace; they must actively pacify it. They do this by adopting the very populist language that the grassroots base uses to demand accountability. The captured class stands at the podium and loudly proclaims "America First," champions "Secure Borders," and explicitly promises "No New Wars."

This high-level campaign rhetoric acts as a psychological lubricant. By telling the public exactly what they want to hear, the captured representatives paralyze the electorate's critical faculties. The citizen thinks, "My representative sounds just like me, so they must be fighting for me," even as that same representative signs off on the $5 Billion parallel funding ledgers for the Abraham Realignment.

The rhetoric of peace is the very camouflage used to normalize kinetic expansion. The "No New Wars" anchor ensures that when Operation Epic Fury is launched, the public is cognitively primed to accept it not as a new war, but as an unavoidable, temporary "security measure" necessary to finally achieve the peace they were promised.

Through the capture of the representative class and the weaponization of populist rhetoric, the Architects ensure that the gates of the people farm remain locked from the inside.

The False Vanguard: The Mechanism of False Hope

To successfully manage a "people farm," the Architects cannot simply build electric fences; they must also provide a pressure valve. When the 56% majority begins to awaken to the $200B Siphon and the suspension of the War Powers Act, their natural instinct is to organize and rebel.

The system anticipates this. Rather than crushing the rebellion outright—which risks creating martyrs—the trans-national shadow state employs the **False Vanguard**.

The Architects allow, and covertly fund, the rise of highly visible "dissidents," alternative media networks, and populist firebrands who loudly attack the peripheral symptoms of the system while fiercely protecting its core architecture. These controlled opposition figures will scream on camera about "woke culture" or "domestic tax rates," but the moment the conversation turns to the $157M Affinity ledgers, the Board of Peace, or the Geneva Sabotage, they deploy the very "thought-terminating clichés" we will discuss in the next section.

The False Vanguard serves to corral the awakened citizens. It gives the grassroots base the illusion that they have a champion fighting for them on the inside, ensuring they remain passive spectators rather than sovereign actors. They sit back and wait for the "plan" to unfold, not realizing their chosen champion is just another manager on the farm, paid to keep them docile while the liquidity is drained.

1.4 The Cognitive Seal: Reflexive Dismissal and the Architecture of Denial

The Psychopathy of Pragmatism (The Architects' Moral Compass)

Before understanding how the public's mind is sealed, one must understand how the Architects justify the seal to themselves. The perpetrators of this shadow architecture do not view their actions as "evil." They operate on a chilling calculus known as the Psychopathy of Pragmatism. They do not wake up intending to be evil; they view themselves as the burdened saviors of an obsolete world. They believe the nation-state is a dangerous relic and that the "people farm" must be strictly managed because the public is too ignorant to survive the complexities of the 21st century. To them, bypassing the War Powers Act and using the Theological Shield isn't treason or blasphemy— it is a "necessary administrative restructuring" for the greater global good. Exposing this cold, utilitarian savior complex makes their actions far more terrifying, as their evil is thoroughly and bureaucratically rationalized.

There is a profound psychological maxim that strikes at the very heart of the "people farm" we have described: It is easier to fool a person than to convince them they have been fooled. The Architects of the Void understand this human frailty perfectly. They know that the Silicon Guard can filter the digital square, and the Captured Class can spout populist rhetoric from the podium, but the ultimate defense mechanism must reside within the minds of the public itself. If the Board of Peace and the $200B liquidity siphon are to operate in the open, the system requires a psychological firewall that prevents the masses from ever asking the right questions.

This firewall is the **Cognitive Seal**.

The Cognitive Seal is not a physical barrier; it is a programmed psychological reflex. It is the architecture of denial that weaponizes a citizen's own ego and peer group against the truth, ensuring that the inmates fiercely defend the bars of their own prison.

The Ego Trap: Weaponized Pride

To convince a person that they have been fooled is to inflict a severe wound to their ego. It requires them to admit that their deeply held beliefs, their political loyalties, and their perception of reality have been expertly manipulated.

The system leverages this natural aversion to intellectual pain. Through constant algorithmic reinforcement, the Silicon Guard creates an environment where trusting the "MAGA Monolith Myth" or the "No New Wars" rhetoric is framed as the ultimate sign of patriotism and intelligence. Conversely, questioning the official narrative—asking why a private equity proxy sits on the Board of Peace, or why the War Powers Act is being bypassed—is framed as a moral and intellectual failure.

When presented with hard evidence of the $157M Affinity fee ledgers or the Geneva Sabotage, the average citizen will not evaluate the data objectively. Their programmed reflex is to protect their ego by instantly rejecting the information.

Reflexive Dismissal and the Thought-Terminating Cliché

The primary mechanism of the Cognitive Seal is Reflexive Dismissal. The Architects have seeded the public consciousness with "thought-terminating clichés"—short, emotionally charged phrases designed to instantly short-circuit critical analysis.

When a researcher points out the glaring discrepancies in the Gaza-First prototype or the consolidation of privateer power, they are met with pre-packaged linguistic weapons:

- "That's just a conspiracy theory."
- "You're being unpatriotic during a time of crisis."
- "That is a dangerous, fringe ideology."

These phrases act as a cognitive kill-switch. The moment one of these labels is applied to a piece of information, the listener's brain is given permission to stop thinking. They do not have to do the difficult work of reading the Board of Peace charter or tracking the foreign fundraising; the thought-terminating cliché has already done the "thinking" for them.

The Theological Quarantine (A Prelude to the Shield)

The most impenetrable layer of this Reflexive Dismissal occurs when the Architects wrap their material theft in sacred or ethnic identities. If a citizen questions the asymmetrical leverage used to launch Operation Epic Fury, they are not just called incorrect—they are reflexively branded with accusations of bigotry, antisemitism, or religious heresy.

This creates a Theological Quarantine. By linking the exposure of financial and geopolitical crimes to profound moral taboos, the system ensures that pointing out the truth becomes a socially fatal act. The citizen's own friends, family, and peers will enforce the quarantine, isolating anyone who dares to speak out. The Silicon Guard does not even have to intervene; the "people farm" polices itself.

The Function of the Seal: Contempt Prior to Investigation

The Cognitive Seal is the ultimate triumph of the Consolidation of the Void. It ensures that all the evidence of the shadow architecture can exist in plain sight—in UN mandates, in SEC filings, and in the Davos Charter—because the Architects know the public has been programmed not to look.

The 18th-century philosopher William Paley famously identified the one principle that is a bar against all information, which is proof against all arguments, and which cannot fail to keep a man in everlasting ignorance: contempt prior to investigation. To condemn a premise before giving it thorough consideration is the literal height of ignorance. Yet, this is exactly what the Silicon Guard and the Captured Class train the public to do. They manufacture contempt for the truth so that the public will never investigate the $200B Siphon.

To break this seal, a standard political awakening is insufficient. Escaping this prison requires a fundamental shift in perception, a willingness to endure the pain of recognizing the deception, and a spiritual grounding strong enough to withstand the isolation of the quarantine.

1.5 The Call for Divine Discernment: The Armor of God and Spiritual Sovereignty

If the Cognitive Seal relies on manufactured contempt and algorithmic gaslighting, it cannot be defeated by logic, political debate, or civic organizing alone. The "people farm" is too well-funded, and the Silicon Guard's biohybrid swarms and World Models are too pervasive. When the digital archive is constantly overwritten via Retroactive Content Injection, historical facts become malleable. When the historical record cannot be trusted, the individual must rely on a higher, immutable frequency of truth.

To confront the sheer scale of the Board of Peace and the trans-national shadow state is to realize a stark, sobering reality: alone, as a single material actor, you cannot defeat this system. But rather than a source of despair, this realization is the beginning of true liberation.

Escaping the Void requires the active cultivation of Divine Discernment and the assumption of spiritual armor.

Principalities and Powers

The administrative capture we have mapped—the private equity ledgers, the $200B Siphon, the captured representative class—is the modern manifestation of an ancient warning. As the Apostle Paul wrote to the Ephesians (6:12): "For we wrestle not against flesh and blood, but against principalities, against powers, against the rulers of the darkness of this world, against spiritual wickedness in high places." The Architects of the Void are these modern principalities. Fighting them on their own terms, using the political levers they already own, leads only to exhaustion and despair. The battle for agency must first be won in the spiritual and cognitive realms.

The Armor of the Mind

Discernment, in this context, is not merely a religious abstraction; it is a tactical necessity. It is the "Mind Armor" required to walk through the semantic triggers ("America First," "No New Wars") without being hypnotized by them. To break the systemic "Fog of War," the individual must adopt three specific practices of discernment:

- **The Suspension of the Ego:** The reader must accept the premise that they have likely been fooled by the "MAGA" Monolith Myth. This requires humility. The ego will fight to maintain the illusion of the 94% consensus because there is comfort in the herd. Discernment demands that one steps out of the herd and evaluates the data (like the $157M Affinity ledgers) without emotional attachment to the political figures involved.
- **Reading the Material Ledger, Not the Rhetoric:** The Architects of the Void speak in the language of the sacred while operating in the profane. Divine discernment requires the individual to completely ignore what

a leader says from the podium and look exclusively at what they fund. If a representative claims to be an isolationist but signs a multi-billion dollar continuing resolution for the "Gaza-First" prototype, discernment immediately identifies the lie.

- **Rejecting the Thought-Terminating Cliché:** The discerning mind must train itself to recognize when a "Reflexive Dismissal" is being deployed. When the media or a peer group brands an investigation into the Board of Peace as a "dangerous conspiracy," the discerning individual recognizes this not as a warning, but as a coordinate—a marker indicating exactly where the truth is hidden.

The Armor of God as Systemic Defense

This necessary Mind Armor is practically applied through the Armor of God (Ephesians 6:13-17) for the era of the Silicon Guard:

- **The Belt of Truth:** In an age of Statistical Mirages and AI-generated consensus, the truth is what holds the rest of your defenses together. It is the uncompromising recognition of material reality.
- **The Breastplate of Righteousness & The Shoes of Peace:** The Board of Peace offers a false, privatized peace built on endless kinetic friction and biometric control. True peace is internal. It is the spiritual grounding that allows you to remain calm and unshaken even as the economic and geopolitical systems around you are intentionally collapsed.
- **The Shield of Faith:** This is the direct countermeasure to the Cognitive Seal and the Theological Quarantine. The system will fire the "fiery darts" of Reflexive Dismissal—calling you a conspiracy theorist, a traitor, or an outcast—to force your compliance. Faith is the shield that quenches these attacks, allowing you to endure the social isolation of seeing the truth.
- **The Helmet of Salvation & The Sword of the Spirit:** The ultimate defense of the mind. The Sword is the active discernment required to cut through semantic triggers and thought-terminating clichés, severing the psychological lubricants used by the Captured Class.

The Reclamation of Intellectual Agency

The Consolidation of the Void relies on the assumption that the public is spiritually and intellectually asleep. The Call for Divine Discernment is the alarm bell. It is the recognition that while the trans-national shadow state can control the digital square, manipulate the World Models, and capture the representative class, it cannot forcibly override the sovereign, discerning mind of an individual who refuses to condemn the truth prior to investigation.

In the World, But Not of It

There is profound comfort in accepting your material limitations in the face of this shadow architecture. Your primary directive is not to single-handedly dismantle the Board of Peace or halt the Gaza-First prototype. Your directive is to refuse their programming, document their deeds, and maintain your spiritual sovereignty.

You are forced to exist geographically within the "people farm," but you do not have to belong to it. You are, as the scripture dictates, "in the world, but not of it" (John 15:19). The geopolitical borders and financial ledgers managed by the Architects are temporary constructs of the Void. Your allegiance, your intellect, and your peace of mind operate under a higher jurisdiction that no biohybrid swarm can map and no Retroactive Content Injection can erase.

With this spiritual sovereignty established, the reader is no longer a passive subject of the illusion. They are a protected witness, ready to walk into the belly of the beast.

2

CHAPTER II: THE SHADOW ARCHITECTURE

2.1 The Geneva Sabotage: The 48-Hour Collapse of State-Led Diplomacy (Feb 26-28)

If the "MAGA" Monolith Myth provides the psychological cover for the transnational shadow state, the events of late February 2026 provide its operational blueprint. To transition from the diplomatic "software" of the previous era into the kinetic "hardware" of Operation Roaring Lion, the Architects required a catalyst. They needed a diplomatic failure so spectacular and public that the resulting military escalation and the $200B liquidity siphon would appear as the only rational alternatives.

The public was told that diplomacy failed. The material reality is that it was systematically assassinated. Geneva was not a negotiation; it was a controlled demolition executed by private envoys over a span of exactly 48 hours.

The Illusion of the Sovereign Table

When the official delegations arrived in Geneva on the morning of February 26, the state-aligned media broadcast an atmosphere of cautious optimism. The official State Department envoys, acting under the traditional purview of the constitutional republic, brought a framework designed to de-escalate regional friction and halt the slide into a broader theater of war.

They were completely unaware that they were participating in a piece of theater. The true negotiations were not happening at the main diplomatic tables; they were occurring in the parallel, unrecorded backchannels managed by the Board of Peace (BoP) proxies and private equity principals.

The 48-Hour Sabotage Timeline

February 26: The Parallel Infiltration

- **0800 Hours (The State Illusion):** Official diplomatic channels open. The standard framework for regional stabilization is presented. The terms are manageable, focusing on traditional statecraft—border recognitions, temporary ceasefire zones, and the return of hostages.
- **1800 Hours (The Backchannel Override):** While the press is focused on the official delegates, the "Unelected Envoys"—representing the interests of the trans-national privateer state and the Sunni Gulf Monarchies—initiate direct, unrecorded communications with key adversarial nodes. These envoys carry no Senate confirmation, yet they wield the asymmetric leverage of global capital.
- **2300 Hours:** The privateers deploy the "Geneva Sabotage." They silently inject extreme, non-negotiable economic poison pills into the periphery of the agreement. These new clauses subtly demand the forfeiture of sovereign development rights, laying the groundwork for the "Eastern Mediterranean Riviera" biometric workforce zones.

February 27: The Term Sheet Substitution

- **1000 Hours (The Financial Ambush):** The adversarial delegations, previously nearing an agreement with the official State Department, are suddenly confronted with the BoP's shadow clauses. The terms have shifted from standard border disputes to total economic and administrative surrender to an unelected international board.
- **1400 Hours:** The official U.S. diplomats are bypassed entirely. When they attempt to clarify the sudden friction, they are compartmentalized by their own intelligence handlers (the "Willful Ignorance" detailed in Chapter I).

The State Department is functionally blind to the fact that private equity proxies have rewritten the rules of engagement overnight.

- **2100 Hours:** The private envoys issue a deliberate ultimatum designed to be rejected. It strips the adversarial leadership of any face-saving exit, ensuring that walking away is their only viable option.

February 28: The Calculated Collapse

- **0400 Hours:** The summit shatters. The adversarial delegations walk out. The official state diplomats are left stunned at the table, unable to explain the sudden, catastrophic breakdown of a deal they thought was secured 24 hours prior.
- **0600 Hours (The Narrative Deployment):** Before the official delegates can even brief their superiors, the Silicon Guard and the Captured Class spring into action. The narrative is instantly solidified across all media platforms: The enemy is entirely to blame. They walked away from a historic peace deal. They only understand force.
- **1200 Hours:** The psychological lubricant is applied. The "No New Wars" politicians solemnly take to the podiums, expressing their deep regret that diplomacy failed, thereby clearing the jurisdictional and moral path for Operation Epic Fury and the forthcoming Operation Roaring Lion.

The Death of Statecraft

The Geneva Sabotage is the ultimate proof of concept for the Consolidation of the Void. It demonstrates that the constitutional republic no longer possesses the agency to make peace. Traditional statecraft has been entirely subverted by the privateer state. By collapsing the talks, the unelected envoys achieved their true objective: guaranteeing the permanent instability required to justify the massive bond issuances, the private reconstruction contracts, and the complete bypass of the War Powers Act.

They did not go to Geneva to prevent a war. They went to Geneva to secure the business model for the Board of Peace.

2.2 The $5 Billion Parallel: Affinity Partners and the Business of Statecraft

While the official State Department delegates were being systematically blinded and outmaneuvered during the Geneva Sabotage, a second, entirely separate track of "diplomacy" was operating in the shadows. This track was not concerned with borders, hostages, or ceasefires. It was concerned with capitalization.

This is the $5 Billion Parallel. To understand the Consolidation of the Void, one must understand that for the privateer state, active combat is not an interruption of business; it is the ultimate fundraising environment.

At the dead center of this parallel track is Affinity Partners, a private equity firm founded by Jared Kushner.

Kushner is the archetype of the "Unelected Envoy" described in Chapter I. Having utilized his proximity to the executive branch to author the diplomatic "software" of the Abraham Accords in 2020, he seamlessly transitioned through the revolving door to monetize that geopolitical access. The heads of these organizations do not operate in ignorance; they operate with absolute, calculated precision.

The Foreign Capitalization of a Privateer

During the exact windows when kinetic escalation in the Middle East was being engineered, and while public rhetoric loudly proclaimed "America First," Affinity Partners was securing massive capital injections from the very foreign powers driving the regional realignment.

The capitalization of Affinity Partners is a masterclass in asymmetric leverage. The fund rapidly secured backing from the sovereign wealth funds of the Sunni Gulf Monarchies—most notably, a massive $2 Billion anchor investment from Saudi Arabia's Public Investment Fund (PIF), controlled by Crown Prince Mohammed bin Salman (MBS), alongside hundreds of millions from the sovereign funds of the UAE and Qatar.

When a former (and highly influential) senior advisor to the President of the United States receives billions from foreign monarchs during a period of active, shifting alliances, it is not a traditional venture capital investment. It is the purchasing of a shadow foreign policy. It is the funding of the Board of

Peace's privateer engine.

The $157M Fee Ledger: The Illusion of Performance

The smoking gun of the $5 Billion Parallel is found not in what Affinity Partners has successfully built, but in how it extracts wealth regardless of its performance. This is exposed by examining the $157M Fee Ledger.

In traditional free-market capitalism, a private equity firm makes its money through the successful deployment of capital and the generation of returns for its investors. Affinity Partners, however, operates under the rules of the Void. By charging standard management fees (typically 2% annually) on billions of dollars in committed capital—much of which remained undeployed for extended periods—the firm generates massive, guaranteed revenue streams.

The $157M represents the estimated management fees siphoned into the privateer ledger without the requirement of bringing a single successful product or service to the American market.

- **The Geopolitical Retainer:** The Sunni monarchs did not pay these fees because they were desperate for Kushner's financial acumen in traditional markets. They paid them as a geopolitical retainer. It ensures that when the "Gaza-First" prototype is built, and when the Board of Peace begins issuing reconstruction contracts, the Gulf Monarchies have a fully paid, highly incentivized proxy whispering in the ear of the American executive branch.

The Convergence of Ledgers

The true horror of the 48-hour Geneva Sabotage is realized when you overlay the diplomatic timeline with the financial ledgers.

While the American public was being algorithmically pacified by the Silicon Guard to accept Operation Epic Fury as a "defense of freedom," the architects of the conflict were actively managing billions in foreign capital from the region. Kushner and the PIF operate with full visibility. They understand that state-led diplomacy must be collapsed so that private-led reconstruction can begin.

The $5 Billion Parallel proves that the "Fog of War" only exists for the citizens trapped inside the people farm. For the privateers, the ledgers are perfectly clear.

2.3 The "Veneer of Credibility": Philanthropy, Real Estate, and the Architecture of the Trans-National Club

The $5 Billion Parallel exposes the raw, unvarnished financial engine of the shadow architecture. However, the Architects of the Void understand a fundamental rule of human psychology: you cannot publicly present a $157M fee ledger extracted from foreign monarchs and call it statecraft. Raw extraction is optically toxic. To operate in the open, the privateer state requires a sophisticated camouflage.

They achieve this by wrapping their geopolitical maneuvers in the culturally untouchable garments of high society. They operate as a trans-national "gang" or exclusive club, washing their leverage through two primary engines of public legitimacy: luxury real estate development and global philanthropy.

The Architecture of the Trans-National Club

How do they get away with it? They get away with it by monopolizing the definition of prestige. The "gang" is a self-reinforcing loop of unelected envoys, private equity principals, and think-tank directors. They sit on the boards of each other's NGOs, they attend the same Davos summits, and they grant each other humanitarian awards.

When a citizen questions the motives of a figure like Kushner or the proxies on the Board of Peace, the system does not defend the financials—it defends the credentials. The Captured Class and the media will point to the individual's philanthropic galas, their real estate portfolios, and their prestigious board seats. This closed loop of mutual validation creates the Veneer of Credibility, a dazzling social shield that blinds the public to the underlying theft of their national sovereignty and agency.

The Ancient Playbook: An Inherited Blueprint

This closed loop is not a modern invention; it is the refinement of an ancient playbook dating back to pre-history. The mechanics of the shadow architecture have not changed; they have merely changed hands and updated their vocabulary to match the era.

Where ancient temple priests hoarded agricultural wealth behind the absolute authority of the divine, and Roman patricians consolidated public lands into private latifundia (see exhibit A for definition) under the guise of stabilizing the Republic, the game plan was the same. Centuries later, the British East India Company acted as the ultimate privateer state, extracting subcontinental wealth while hiding behind the philanthropic shield of a "civilizing mission."

Today's trans-national club is simply the latest inheritor of this blueprint. They have replaced the "divine right of kings" with the "mandate of international reconstruction," but the core strategy remains unbroken: consolidate material wealth and jurisdictional control while maintaining an absolute monopoly on the era's highest moral virtues.

The Jurisdictional Veil: The Shield of Legal Immunity

The trans-national club does not rely on social prestige alone; the Veneer of Credibility serves a critical, mechanical legal function. The Architects utilize these philanthropic and international frameworks to drape themselves in a Jurisdictional Veil.

When statecraft is privatized and moved into the hands of international NGOs, UN-backed "Peace Boards," and trans-national equity funds, it is deliberately moved completely outside the jurisdiction of the constitutional republic. By operating in this stateless void, the privateers bypass Freedom of Information Act (FOIA) requests, congressional subpoenas, and domestic financial audits. A citizen cannot audit a private equity ledger in the same way they can audit a State Department budget. The "club" uses the architecture of global charity to grant themselves the ultimate sovereign immunity, ensuring their extraction remains legally invisible.

Luxury Real Estate: Jurisdictional Capture in Plain Sight

To the uninitiated, luxury real estate is simply a marker of wealth. To the Architects, it is the ultimate tool for jurisdictional capture.

When state-led diplomacy is sabotaged (as seen in Geneva) and kinetic military operations clear a region, the resulting devastation is not viewed by the privateers as a tragedy; it is viewed as a zoning opportunity. We see this manifested in the conceptualization of the "Eastern Mediterranean Riviera."

By purchasing massive tracts of strategically vital land under the guise of "luxury development" and "economic revitalization," the privateers achieve a bloodless conquest.

- **The Erasure of Sovereignty:** Sovereign land, once governed by the people who lived on it, is transitioned into a privatized asset class.
- **The Tenant Paradigm:** The organic citizens are displaced, and the new inhabitants are no longer citizens with constitutional rights; they are corporate tenants subject to the terms of service dictated by the developers and the sovereign wealth funds that financed them.

The real estate front allows the Architects to literally redraw the maps of nations without ever formally declaring a war of acquisition. They just call it a "master-planned community."

The Kinetic Subcontract: Taxpayer-Funded Demolition

There remains a glaring mechanical gap between the diplomatic collapse in Geneva and the construction of the "Eastern Mediterranean Riviera." How do the Architects actually clear the land? The ultimate asymmetric leverage of the trans-national club is that they never pay for their own overhead. Through the Kinetic Subcontract, the privateers use the constitutional republic's military apparatus as a free, publicly-funded demolition crew.

When the Geneva Sabotage triggers kinetic escalations like Operation Epic Fury, the American taxpayer funds the multi-billion-dollar munitions, the logistics, and the physical clearing of the region. The citizens of the "people farm" bear the total financial and moral cost of the destruction. The soldiers on the ground operate under the illusion that they are fighting a sovereign war for national security. But to the Architects of the Board of Peace, the military is unwittingly serving as a publicly-funded site-preparation crew. Once the military clears the "zoning area" at the taxpayers' expense, the private equity firms sweep in with their philanthropic Veneer of Credibility to claim the newly available land. The system is perfectly optimized: socialize the demolition, privatize the development.

The Philanthropic Shield: Weaponized Humanitarianism

The most insidious layer of the Veneer of Credibility is the weaponization of charity. As the kinetic friction of Operation Epic Fury tears down the physical and social infrastructure of a region, the very same private equity networks that funded the political architects of the war pivot to become the "saviors."

They launch massive, billion-dollar "Reconstruction Funds" and humanitarian NGOs.

- **The "Gaza-First" Prototype:** When they deploy capital to rebuild, they do not rebuild the sovereign nation that existed before. They use the philanthropic mandate to build the infrastructure of the "people farm."
- **Biometric Compliance:** Humanitarian aid and reconstruction dollars are made contingent upon the implementation of total biometric surveillance, digital ID grids, and centralized digital currencies.

If anyone dares to criticize this totalitarian control grid, the Architects simply point to their philanthropic charter. "How can you criticize us?" they ask. "We are building schools. We are providing relief." The Philanthropic Shield uses the moral high ground to enforce absolute administrative servitude.

The Illusion of the Good Manager

Ultimately, the Veneer of Credibility is what makes the Cognitive Seal (detailed in Chapter I) possible. The public is desperate to believe that the people in charge are fundamentally good. By hiding the $200B liquidity siphon behind the glossy brochures of luxury real estate and the tear-inducing marketing of global philanthropy, the Architects allow the public to sleep peacefully, confident that "the gang" has everything under control.

They are not viewed as privateers strip-mining the republic; they are heralded as visionary developers and benevolent philanthropists leading humanity into a new era of managed peace.

The Calculus of Apathy: Why They Do Not Fear Disclosure

How, then, do the current operators navigate around those attempting to disclose this reality—the researchers, the whistleblowers, and the authors of volumes such as this?

The chilling truth is that, by and large, they do not care. They do not view full disclosure as an existential threat because they operate on the Calculus of Apathy. In the eyes of the Architects, even if the people are smart enough to understand the game plan, the people are structurally powerless to stop it.

The privateers rely on Asymmetric Leverage. They know that understanding the $157M fee ledger or the Geneva Sabotage requires no small amount of intellectual rigor, but stopping it requires multi-billion-dollar capital structures, military coordination, and algorithmic dominance—tools the grassroots public does not possess. They view dissidents as screaming into a void. They are entirely confident that the Silicon Guard will suppress the reach of the disclosure, and the Veneer of Credibility will ultimately soothe the broader masses back to sleep. Their arrogance is their armor; they believe the "people farm" is too thoroughly managed for the truth to ever mobilize into a kinetic threat.

2.4 The Emergency Ledger: Legislative Bypass and the Invisible Tax

We have mapped the diplomatic sabotage, the private capitalization, and the physical clearing of the land. But a final, critical mechanical gap remains in this economic analysis. If the 56% majority actively opposes these kinetic escalations, and the government is extracting a $200B Siphon to fund the Kinetic Subcontract, why is there no immediate, massive taxpayer revolt?

The Architects know they cannot raise domestic income taxes to fund Operation Epic Fury; direct taxation would trigger an immediate rebellion on the "people farm." Instead, the extraction is executed entirely in the shadows through the **Emergency Ledger**.

The Legislative Bypass: The Omnibus Extortion

To move $200 Billion without public consent, the Captured Class must completely bypass standard congressional budgetary order. They achieve this by declaring the results of the Geneva Sabotage a sudden "global crisis" that requires immediate, unquestioned funding.

The vehicle for this theft is the "Emergency Supplemental Appropriation."

These are massive, thousand-page omnibus bills drafted in the dark by uniparty leadership and unelected committee staffers. They are forced onto the legislative floor hours before a deadline, passed under the manufactured, apocalyptic threat of a government shutdown. The Captured Class claims they are voting to "keep the government open" or "support the troops," when in reality, they are authorizing the blank checks required by the Board of Peace. The constitutional power of the purse is circumvented by the politics of extortion.

Central Bank Monetization: The Engine of the Siphon

However, the treasury does not actually possess the $200 Billion required to fund these emergency ledgers. Because these parallel funding tracks are entirely deficit-financed, they require the ultimate tool of the trans-national shadow state: the complicity of the central bank.

To fund the Kinetic Subcontract, the central bank simply monetizes the newly issued sovereign debt. They conjure the required billions out of the digital ether, expanding the monetary base to pay the defense contractors and the privateer proxies.

Inflation: The Invisible Tax

The true brilliance—and horror—of the Emergency Ledger is how the bill is ultimately delivered to the public. The cost of the $200B Siphon is passed to the citizen not on April 15th, but through **inflation**.

Inflation is the ultimate "Invisible Tax" of the shadow architecture. When the monetary supply is diluted to fund foreign kinetic operations, the purchasing power of every dollar held by the grassroots public is mathematically reduced. The citizen unknowingly pays for the multi-billion-dollar munitions and the clearing of the "Eastern Mediterranean Riviera" every time they purchase groceries, fill their gas tank, or pay their utility bills.

The Perfect Closed Loop

This mechanism perfectly optimizes the "people farm." The Architects drain the wealth of the republic through the silent theft of purchasing power, ensuring the citizens are kept too economically exhausted and distracted by domestic survival to fight back against the geopolitical theft occurring overseas. The Emergency Ledger closes the loop of the shadow architecture: the citizens are forced to silently finance the very trans-national engine that is systematically stripping them of their sovereignty.

The Spiritual Bounty: Finding Agency in a Lawless Land

When a citizen first peers through the Jurisdictional Veil and comprehends the Calculus of Apathy, the natural resulting emotion is a profound sense of hopelessness. To realize you are living in a functionally lawless land—managed by privateers while the masses fight over the material scraps of a rigged system—is to experience the death of a deeply held delusion. Millions remain trapped in this delusion, exhausting their energy believing they still have a voice in the fight or a representative who will suddenly reform the system from within.

But the Architects' greatest miscalculation is believing that the material ledger is the only measure of wealth.

While the shadow architecture systematically strips the republic of its material scraps, a profound Spiritual Bounty remains untouched and infinitely available. This realization is not meant to make the reader feel hopelessly lost in a dystopian machine; it is meant to make them feel found.

Once you stop fighting for a seat at a table that was built to consume you, you reclaim your true agency. The disillusionment is the cure. You are no longer a deluded participant in a theater of managed democracy; you are a clear-eyed witness operating under a higher, sovereign jurisdiction. The system can capture the land, rewrite the digital archive, and siphon the treasury, but it cannot tax, algorithmically alter, or seize the spiritual sovereignty of an awakened mind. In the shadow of a lawless land, this spiritual bounty is the ultimate unseizable asset.

3

CHAPTER III: THE SYNAGOGUE OF SATAN

3.1 The Architecture of Spiritual Imposters (Revelation 2:9 and 3:9)

The $200B Siphon, the Geneva Sabotage, and the construction of the "people farm" are material crimes, but they are driven by a spiritual engine. The trans-national club cannot sustain its global extraction through kinetic force and financial ledgers alone; it requires an absolute monopoly on moral and spiritual authority. To achieve this, the Architects must wear the garments of the righteous.

This mechanism of deception was explicitly identified in the biblical texts, serving as a timeless warning against institutionalized spiritual fraud. In the Book of Revelation (2:9 and 3:9), the text issues a stark condemnation of those *"which say they are Jews, and are not, but are the synagogue of Satan."*

To the undiscerning mind, this passage is often misread through a narrow, strictly historical, or ethnic lens. But the trans-national shadow state operates on a frequency that is *so much bigger than that.* To understand the "Synagogue of Satan" in the era of the Silicon Guard and the Board of Peace, one must deconstruct the terms:

- **The Synagogue (The Assembly):** A synagogue is not merely a building; it is an assembly, a structured organization of governance, law, and shared worship. In the modern context, this assembly is the "club" detailed in Chapter II—the Davos summits, the Board of Peace, the interlocking directorates of global NGOs, and the private equity roundtables.

- **Satan (The Adversary):** In the original Hebrew, *ha-satan* translates literally to "the accuser" or "the adversary." It is the spirit of opposition to divine sovereignty and human agency.
- **"Say they are... and are not" (The False Mandate):** In the biblical context, to be a Jew was to be a member of the covenant—the chosen stewards of God's law, truth, and moral light. The text warns of an assembly that *claims* this sacred stewardship, that *claims* to be the moral authority of the world, but is actually operating as an adversarial force of enslavement.

The Synagogue of Satan is the ultimate realization of the "Veneer of Credibility." It is a global assembly of spiritual imposters. They claim to be the saviors, the peacekeepers, and the chosen stewards of the earth, but their true master is the Void.

3.2 Claiming to be What They Are Not: The Secular Priesthood

How does this ancient warning map onto the modern geopolitical landscape? The trans-national club operates as a secular priesthood, demanding the blind faith of the masses while systematically violating every tenet of the covenant they claim to uphold.

They claim to be what they are not through three primary inversions of truth:

1. They Claim the Mandate of Peace (But Serve Kinetic Friction)

The assembly names its instruments with sacred vocabulary—"The Board of Peace," "The Abraham Realignment," "Humanitarian Corridors." They present themselves as the only adults in the room, the enlightened diplomats uniquely qualified to save the world from itself.

- *The Reality:* As proven by the Geneva Sabotage, they are the very architects of the conflict. They use the rhetoric of peace to secure the multi-billion-dollar Kinetic Subcontract, feeding the military-industrial complex and the private reconstruction ledgers. They are not peacemakers; they are war-managers.

2. They Claim the Mandate of Stewardship (But Serve Extraction)

Through their philanthropic shields and environmental, social, and governance (ESG) mandates, the assembly claims to be the righteous stewards of the earth. They dictate how the grassroots public must live, what energy they are permitted to consume, and how their sovereign lands must be managed to "save the planet."

- *The Reality:* They view the earth not as a creation to be stewarded, but as an asset class to be zoned. They leverage these environmental and humanitarian mandates to bankrupt independent agriculture, centralize supply chains, and build the "Eastern Mediterranean Riviera" on the ruins of sovereign nations. They are not stewards; they are liquidators.

3. They Claim the Mandate of Truth (But Serve the Illusion)

The trans-national club funds the fact-checking apparatus, the algorithm filters of the Silicon Guard, and the "World Models" of artificial intelligence. They claim to be the definitive arbiters of reality, protecting the public from "disinformation."

- *The Reality:* They are the authors of the "MAGA Monolith Myth" and the masters of Retroactive Content Injection. They eradicate historical truth to protect their ledgers, operating entirely on the deception of the masses.

3.3 The Rituals of the Adversary: The Worship of the Ledger

If this trans-national network is a "synagogue," then it must have a religion, an altar, and a ritual.

The religion of the Architects is **Total Information Awareness and Com-**

plete Administrative Control. They do not worship a transcendent Creator who grants human beings inherent, unalienable rights. They worship the consolidation of power within the Void. In their theology, the human being is not a sovereign soul; the human being is a data point, a biological variable to be managed, taxed, and algorithmically predicted.

Their rituals are not performed with incense or hymns; they are performed through the mechanics of the "people farm":

- **The Ritual of the Emergency Ledger:** The silent, continuous extraction of the republic's wealth through inflation and omnibus extortion.
- **The Ritual of Biometric Compliance:** Forcing the global populace to submit to digital IDs, central bank digital currencies (CBDCs), and social credit gateways to participate in society. It is the modern manifestation of bowing to the idol.
- **The Ritual of the Theological Quarantine:** Whenever their financial and geopolitical crimes are exposed, the assembly reflexively hides behind sacred identities. They scream "antisemitism," "bigotry," or "heresy" to socially destroy anyone who dares to shine a light on the $157M fee ledgers. They use the sacred as a human shield for the profane.

The Synagogue of Satan is not a hidden cabal in a dark room; it is the fully visible, institutionalized architecture of global governance that calls good evil, and evil good. They claim the mantle of divine right to justify a system of absolute, adversarial tyranny.

The Law of Manufactured Consent: The Vampire's Invitation

If the trans-national network commands such vast material wealth and kinetic leverage, a profound cosmic question remains: why do they spend billions on the Silicon Guard, algorithmic gaslighting, and the Veneer of Credibility instead of utilizing raw, brute force to physically enslave the populace?

The answer lies in a foundational spiritual law binding the Adversary: the law of human free will. In both biblical theology and esoteric tradition, the Adversary cannot forcibly seize a sovereign soul or its earthly jurisdiction; it must be surrendered. The vampire cannot enter the house unless he is invited.

If the trans-national club simply marched armies into the streets to violently chain the masses, it would violate this cosmic law and instantly awaken the righteous spiritual resistance of the public. Therefore, the entire shadow architecture exists for one ultimate spiritual purpose: **to manufacture your consent.**

They do not just want your wealth; they need you to willingly hand it to them by voting for the Captured Class. They do not just want your biometric data; they need you to click "Accept" on the terms and conditions of their digital IDs in the name of convenience. They engineer the economic exhaustion and the harvest of "loosh" (see appendix A for definition) so that when they finally present the ultimate chains—central bank digital currencies (CBDCs) and a global social credit grid—the masses will be so desperate for relief that they will willingly beg for the collar.

By tricking the "people farm" into choosing the Broad Way, the Architects attempt to absolve themselves of the spiritual crime of theft. In their twisted, legalistic framework, it is not slavery if the livestock walks into the pen and locks the gate themselves. This revelation, however, places the ultimate power back in the hands of the reader: if the system requires your consent to operate, then simply withholding your consent breaks their legal hold over you.

3.4 The Occult Engine: Dominion, Blood, and the False Light

To fully comprehend the operational capacity of the Synagogue of Satan, one must ask the foundational legal and spiritual question: *How does the Adversary possess the authority to orchestrate this global architecture in the first place?* He possesses it because it was legally surrendered to him.

The biblical narrative establishes that the sovereign dominion over the earth was originally granted to mankind. At the Fall, through the deception in the Garden, humanity abdicated that jurisdictional authority, handing the "title deed" of the earth to the Adversary. This is why Christ explicitly referred to Satan as the "prince of this world" (John 14:30), and why the Adversary could legitimately offer the kingdoms of the world to Christ in the desert (Matthew

4:8-9)—because, temporarily and materially, he held the keys.

The trans-national club, the Architects of the Void, operate under this hijacked earthly jurisdiction. They are the mortal managers of this stolen dominion. And because they serve this ancient principality, they are bound to enact its ancient rituals, merely updated for the 21st century.

Lucifer: The Illumination of the Void

At the apex of this spiritual hierarchy is Lucifer, the "light-bringer." The greatest deception of the Synagogue of Satan is that it rarely presents itself as darkness; it presents itself as illumination.

Luciferian ideology is fundamentally the promise of omniscience and godhood without submission to the Creator. In the modern era, this "false light" is literally and figuratively the glowing screens of the Silicon Guard. The $1.03 Billion "World Models" and the transhumanist drive for total biometric surveillance are the ultimate technological manifestations of the Luciferian promise: the desire to become all-knowing, all-seeing, and immortal through human engineering. The Architects believe they are bringing the "light" of perfect administrative order to a chaotic world, blinding the masses to the reality of their enslavement.

The Ancient Pantheon in Modern Suits: Baal, Moloch, and Asteroth

Beneath the False Light operate the specialized principalities. The occult traditions and ancient grimoires (such as the Ars Goetia; see appendix A) number these fallen entities at 72, each commanding legions and governing specific domains of human vice. While the modern secular mind dismisses these names as primitive myths, the Architects perform their exact rituals in broad daylight under the guise of geopolitics and economics.

- **Baal (The Lord of Usury and Material Extraction):** The ancient worship of Baal centered on the absolute subjugation of the populace to secure agricultural and material wealth. Today, the altars of Baal are the central banks and the $157M fee ledgers. The $200B Siphon and the debt-enslavement of the Emergency Ledger are modern oblations to the spirit of usury—a system designed to extract the labor and wealth of the "people farm" to enrich the trans-national priesthood.

- **Moloch (The Sacrifice of the Future):** Moloch was the deity who demanded the ultimate price for societal prosperity and security: the sacrifice of the children in the fire. The Architects serve Moloch through the Kinetic Subcontract. What is Operation Epic Fury—or any endless, manufactured war—if not the systemic, kinetic sacrifice of the nation's youth to secure the geopolitical and financial dominance of the elite? Furthermore, the crushing, multi-trillion-dollar sovereign debt layered onto the unborn is the economic equivalent of passing the next generation through the fire.

- **Asteroth (The Corruption of the Mind and Flesh):** Known historically for intellectual corruption and the degradation of natural human design, this principality thrives in the psychological warfare of the Cognitive Seal. The deliberate destruction of objective truth, the algorithmic promotion of societal decay via the Silicon Guard, and the weaponization of human identity are the modern tributes to this spirit of inversion.

The Currency of the Void: Life in the Blood and the Harvest of "Loosh"

Ultimately, the most chilling aspect of the Synagogue of Satan is its adherence to the darkest of all spiritual violations: the extraction of life force.

Leviticus 17:11 states unequivocally: *"For the life of the flesh is in the blood."* Because the Creator placed the sacred essence of mortal life within the blood, the biblical law strictly forbade its consumption or misuse. The occult inversion of this law is the belief that one can capture, consume, or extend one's own power by harvesting the life force of others.

The Architects operate on a macro-systemic version of this vampirism.

- **Kinetic Bloodletting:** The endless regional wars generated by the Board of Peace are not just profitable real estate ventures; they are systemic bloodletting. The kinetic friction generates the chaos, trauma, and literal sacrifice required to keep the trans-national machine fed and the "people farm" in a state of perpetual fear.

- **The Harvest of Loosh:** Beyond physical blood, the principalities feed on the metaphysical energy of human suffering—an energetic currency esoterically referred to as "loosh." The system is intentionally designed to be an engine of despair. The algorithmic terror of the 24/7 news cycle, the engineered economic exhaustion of the Invisible Tax, and the psychological isolation of the Cognitive Seal are not accidental byproducts; they are the harvest. When the citizens of the republic are trapped in a state of perpetual anxiety, division, and hopelessness, they emit the exact frequency of negative spiritual energy that sustains the parasitic entities the Architects serve.

- **The Biometric Harvest:** In their pursuit of transhumanism and radical life extension, the elite increasingly view the biological data, the genetics, and the very physical essence of the populace as raw materials to be mined. They seek to extend their own dominion in the flesh because they have entirely severed themselves from the eternal life of the Spirit.

The Ultimate Price: Gaining the World and Losing the Soul

When one beholds the staggering scope of this trans-national dominance—the wealth of Affinity Partners, the uniparty compliance, the total surveillance grid of the Silicon Guard—it is easy to view the Architects as the ultimate victors of the earthly realm. But this observation misses the fundamental tragedy of their existence. It begs the most devastating question in the biblical canon, recorded in Mark 8:36:

"For what shall it profit a man, if he shall gain the whole world, and lose his own soul?"

The privateers, the captured politicians, and the unelected envoys are not masters; they are the most thoroughly enslaved entities on the board. They have accepted a Faustian bargain. In exchange for seventy or eighty years of material wealth, exclusive board seats, and temporary geopolitical leverage, they have traded the eternal sovereignty of their own souls.

To serve the Synagogue of Satan requires the active, repeated severing of one's conscience. The "Psychopathy of Pragmatism" we mapped in Chapter I is not a sign of intellectual superiority; it is the necrotic symptom of a spiritually dead vessel. They are hollowed out, entirely possessed by the parasitic systems they manage.

Their frantic, multi-billion-dollar investments into life-extension technologies, AI World Models, and transhumanist bunkers are not driven by a visionary love for humanity. They are driven by absolute, paralyzing terror. Subconsciously, the Architects know their dominion is strictly temporary. They know that when the flesh fails, their ledgers cannot buy them out of the jurisdiction of the Creator. They are building a digital, biometric prison on earth because it is the only kingdom they will ever inherit.

To the awakened citizen, the Architects are not to be envied, and ultimately, they are not to be feared. They are to be recognized for what they are: bankrupt souls managing a fading empire of dust. To look at the World Economic Forum, the Board of Peace, or the private equity proxies and see only "greedy politicians" is to miss the entire plot. They are the willing executives of the Adversary's dominion, operating a trans-national Synagogue that demands the wealth of Baal, the blood of Moloch, and the false, glowing light of Lucifer.

3.5 The Path of the Sovereign: The Narrow Gate and the Inversion of Sacrifice

We have exposed the Synagogue of Satan, mapped its ancient principalities, and documented its insatiable extraction of the republic's material and spiritual wealth. But the diagnosis of darkness is only half the equation; the Sovereign must also possess the cure.

If the trans-national club operates on the parasitic principle of sacrificing the populace to preserve the power of the elite, the ultimate counter-measure is found in the exact inversion of that dynamic: the historical and spiritual example of Jesus Christ.

The Inversion of Sacrifice

The Architects of the Void demand the blood of the youth (through the Kinetic Subcontract) and the energetic exhaustion of the masses (the harvest of "loosh") to build their temporary, biometric empires. They use humanity as a consumable resource.

Christ presented the antithesis of the privateer state. He possessed absolute, legitimate dominion over the earth, yet He did not use it to subjugate the "people farm." Instead, the true Sovereign willingly offered Himself as the ultimate sacrifice to pay the debt of the masses. He did not extract life from His followers to extend His own; He poured out His own blood so that His followers might inherit eternal agency. To walk the path of the Sovereign is to recognize that true authority is not measured by how many you can control, but by how much you are willing to lay down for the truth.

Foreknowledge and the Narrow Gate

Christ did not walk into the crucifixion blindly, nor did He ever promise a comfortable, friction-free existence for those who chose to follow Him. He possessed absolute foreknowledge of the betrayal, the mock trials of the captured legal class, and the physical agony that awaited Him.

He imparted this same sober foreknowledge to His followers, issuing a direct warning that applies perfectly to the era of the Silicon Guard and the MAGA Monolith Myth:

"Enter ye in at the strait gate: for wide is the gate, and broad is the way, that leadeth to destruction, and many there be which go in thereat: Because strait is the gate, and narrow is the way, which leadeth unto life, and few there be that find it." (Matthew 7:13-14)

- **The Broad Way:** This is the algorithmically pacified consensus of the "people farm." It is the path of least resistance. It requires only that a citizen accepts the Veneer of Credibility, submits to the Theological Quarantine, and bows to the idols of convenience and biometric compliance. It is comfortable, socially acceptable, and heavily populated. It leads directly into the Void.
- **The Narrow Gate:** This is the path of Spiritual Sovereignty. It requires the shedding of ego, the loss of social prestige, and the willingness to look at the terrifying reality of the $157M fee ledgers without flinching. It is a path of isolation, mockery, and intense spiritual warfare.

When a citizen is branded a heretic, a traitor, or an outcast by the Captured Class for speaking the truth, they must not despair. That isolation is not a sign of failure; it is the definitive proof that they have successfully found the Narrow Gate.

The Final Double-Check: Securing the Sovereign Baseline

Before we move forward to examine the final, technological mechanisms of the Architects' control grid, the Sovereign must perform a final double-check of their own internal architecture. The path forward requires absolute clarity. All bases must be covered:

- **The Material Baseline:** Have you accepted that the material ledger is rigged? You cannot defeat the $200B Siphon using the financial tools owned by the Board of Peace. The Sovereign must detach their sense of security from the trans-national economic grid and root it in divine providence.
- **The Cognitive Baseline:** Have you rejected the False Light? You must commit to continuous Divine Discernment, refusing to be hypnotized by the "America First" or "No New Wars" rhetoric spouted by those actively funding the kinetic destruction.
- **The Spiritual Baseline:** Have you accepted the cost? The Architects sold their souls for the world. The Sovereign must be willing to lose the world to keep their soul.

With this spiritual bounty secured, the delusion is entirely broken. The reader is no longer a victim wandering in a lawless land. They are a fully armored Sovereign, walking the Narrow Way, ready to look directly into the mechanical heart of the beast.

4

CHAPTER IV: THE ECONOMIC ENGINE

4.1 The $200B Siphon: The Executive Bypass and the Drainage of National Liquidity

The "dis-ease" of the modern republic is most clinically observed in its ledgers. To identify the sickness, one must follow the movement of the life-blood of the nation: its liquidity. While the "Silicon Guard" saturates the digital airwaves with narratives of "defending democracy," the material reality is a calculated, multi-generational theft.

This is the **$200B Siphon**—a sophisticated financial vacuum designed to bypass constitutional checkpoints and drain the national treasury into the "Void."

The Jurisdictional Loophole: "Emergency Stability Operations"

The primary mechanism of the siphon is the semantic reclassification of war. Under the U.S. Constitution, the power to declare war rests solely with the people's representatives. However, the Architects have engineered a **War Powers Bypass**.

By labeling kinetic strikes and regional demolitions as **"Emergency Stability Operations" (ESOs)**, the Executive Branch effectively places these actions outside the jurisdiction of the War Powers Act.

44

- **The Bypass:** This allows the Board of Peace (BoP) proxies within the administration to deploy munitions and personnel without a single vote from Congress.
- **The Funding:** On February 19, 2026, the BoP inaugural meeting formalized this bypass, utilizing the "Emergency" designation to pledge an initial **$10 Billion** as a down payment on a projected **$200 Billion** total siphon.
- **The Result:** The legislative branch is reduced to a "Captured Class," tasked only with the ministerial duty of "funding the mission" they did not authorize to fight.

The Banking Cartel: Privatized Reward, Socialized Risk

To understand the Siphon, one must identify its primary mechanical partner: the **Tier-1 Banking Cartel**. These institutions operate behind the **Cognitive Seal**, the programmed blindness that prevents the public from seeing a war as a business transaction.

The **"Too Big to Fail"** doctrine is the financial manifestation of this seal. It creates a system where the bankers take 100% of the rewards from high-risk geopolitical gambles (like the **$5 Billion Parallel; see appendix A**), while passing 100% of the catastrophic risk to the public.

- **The Mechanism:** When the BoP requires $200 Billion for "Stability Operations," the banks do not lend their own capital. They facilitate the issuance of sovereign debt.
- **The Trap:** If the operation succeeds, the private equity principals and the banks reap management fees and interest. If the operation fails, the banks are "bailed out" by the very taxpayers whose liquidity they already siphoned.

The Invisible Tax: Inflation as a Weapon

The $200B Siphon requires the active participation of the central banking system to monetize the debt. Because the treasury is already insolvent, this capital is "asked" for in the form of new debt.

The "Ask": The Architects "ask" the central bank to print the digital liquidity required to fund the munitions.

The "Find": The citizen "finds" the cost of this siphon not in their tax return, but in the grocery store and the utility bill.

Inflation is the **Invisible Tax of the Shadow Architecture**. By diluting the currency to fund the **Kinetic Subcontract**, the system effectively steals the labor and the time of the Remnant to pay for the bombs that clear the land for the "Eastern Mediterranean Riviera." It is a mandatory tithe extracted without the citizen ever clicking "Accept."

The Call to Seek: Reclaiming the Sovereign Baseline

The biblical mandate to **"Seek and ye shall find"** is the individual's first line of defense. The Sovereign must recognize that they are being used as the **Risk-Bearer of Last Resort**. In the eyes of the Architects, you are not a stakeholder; you are the collateral.

When you knock on the door of this understanding, the "Too Big to Fail" illusion shatters. Reclaiming your agency means moving your spiritual and material treasure out of the path of this socialized risk. You cannot be "well" while your life-force is being used as the security for the privateer's next $157M fee ledger.

4.2 The Gaza-First Prototype: The "Eastern Mediterranean Riviera" and the Architecture of Workforce Housing

The physical manifestation of the Board of Peace (BoP) charter is not found in diplomatic treaties; it is found in zoning laws. To understand the Economic Engine, the Sovereign must look past the geopolitical theater and examine the real estate ledgers. The **"Gaza-First" prototype** is the ultimate beta test for **Disaster Capitalism on Steroids**. It is the material proof that the Kinetic Subcontract—funded by the $200B Siphon—is functioning exactly as designed: as a publicly subsidized demolition crew for private equity developers.

The Historical Precedent: The Architecture of Displacement

The strategy of using destruction to bypass property rights is a refined playbook. The tragedy of the masses serves as the acquisition strategy of the elite:

- **The English Enclosure Acts (17th–19th Century):** The original "Blank Slate" maneuver. The state abolished the "Open Field" system, revoking the rights of commoners to live on the land. They legally reclassified "Common Land" as "Waste Land," consolidating small parcels into massive, privately owned estates.
- **The Haussmannization of Paris (1853–1870):** Under the guise of "public health," Baron Haussmann demolished the organic, working-class neighborhoods of Paris to build boulevards for the elite, creating a "debt-balloon" of 2.5 billion francs—a precursor to the modern siphon.
- **The Doctrine of Lapse (British East India Company):** A clinical example of **Jurisdictional Capture**. The Company asserted that any princely state without a natural heir "lapsed" into Company rule, using a **privateer legal formula** to annex millions of square miles.
- **Post-Civil War Reconstruction:** Financial syndicates leveraged devastation to buy assets for "pennies on the dollar."
- **Lahaina, Malibu, and Grizzly Flats (2025):** Developers arrived before the ashes cooled; draconian codes and permitting fees created a financial wall to prevent original owners from rebuilding.

The "Eastern Mediterranean Riviera": Conquest by Development

The Architects of the Void view the devastated coastlines of the Middle East as **distressed assets**. The master plan for the **"Eastern Mediterranean Riviera"** reveals the true, unvarnished objective of **Operation Epic Fury**.

By clearing the land under the unquestionable guise of national security and counter-terrorism, the trans-national club secures miles of prime, strategically vital Mediterranean beachfront. The land is not returned to a sovereign state; it is transferred to the management of the sovereign wealth funds and privateer proxies who financed the **$5 Billion Parallel**. This is the ultimate "value-unlock"—the systemic erasure of a nation, rebranded and rebuilt as an exclusive, trans-national resort and commercial hub.

The Tenant Paradigm: Biometric Workforce Housing

A luxury economic zone requires a servile, highly managed labor force. The organic, displaced populations are not "liberated"; they are corralled into high-density **"workforce housing units"** on the periphery of the Riviera. These are administrative enclosures.

- **The Biological Tether:** Access to the enclave requires digital IDs tied to physical markers.
- **The Financial Tether:** Wages and aid are distributed exclusively via programmable **Central Bank Digital Currencies (CBDCs)**, ensuring the BoP can dictate exactly what the population can buy, where they can travel, and what behavior is permitted.

The organic citizen is reduced to a trackable biological asset. This is the perfection of the **Tenant Paradigm**: you will own nothing, you will be biometrically monitored, and you will labor for the very Architects who financed the destruction of your home.

The Command to Knock: Dismantling the Philanthropic Shield

The system demands the global public passively accept the media narrative that this reconstruction is an act of supreme global charity. But the Sovereign is commanded to actively pierce this illusion: **"Ask, and it shall be given you; seek, and ye shall find; knock, and it shall be opened unto you." (Matthew 7:7).**

- You must **ask** who holds the underlying title to the newly cleared land.
- You must **seek** the truth hidden beneath the rubble, recognizing that the destruction was a prerequisite for the acquisition.
- You must **knock** aggressively on the doors of these "reconstruction" NGOs until the facade falls away, revealing not peacekeepers, but property managers and biometric wardens.

4.3 The Reconstruction Trap: GRAD Funds, the matrix of yield, and the retail complicity of Peace Bonds

The final mechanism of the Economic Engine is not the bomb; it is the bond. Once the land has been "recommissioned," the Architects force the displaced public—and the global taxpayer—to finance the construction of their own enclosure. This is the Reconstruction Trap, operating on the truth of Proverbs 22:7: "The rich ruleth over the poor, and the borrower is servant to the lender."

The Physical Enclosure: The "Project Sunrise" Blueprint

To understand the nature of the financial trap, one must first examine the physical architecture being financed. The transition from military demolition to corporate development is not a pivot; it is a continuous, integrated process. "Project Sunrise" represents the explicit commercial blueprint for the territory—a $112 billion initiative that utilizes the kinetic clearing of the land as a prerequisite for establishing a highly controlled, technologically enclosed real estate asset. It is the physical manifestation of the control grid, operating under the guise of humanitarian reconstruction.

This spatial restructuring relies on three fundamental mechanisms:

I. The Erasure of Northern Urban Centers (The Blank Slate)

The military partition of the territory serves a specific zoning objective. The historical urban centers of the north are not slated for reconstruction; they are scheduled for permanent erasure.

- **Corporate Rezoning:** The organic, historical footprint of the northern cities is being permanently overwritten to create expansive, unpopulated industrial and agricultural zones. This includes the installation of massive

AI data centers and green-energy infrastructure, secured by international military perimeters.

- **The Annihilation of History:** By completely flattening and then rezoning the north, the privateer class achieves a total "value-unlock." The previous property rights, historical claims, and cultural architecture are vaporized, leaving a legally and physically sterile environment ready for corporate development.

II. The High-Density Quadrant Model (Spatial Containment)

To clear the north and the valuable Mediterranean coastline, the surviving population must be geographically consolidated. The "New Gaza" vision explicitly outlines the relocation of the displaced into four isolated, high-density residential "quadrants" in the south.

- **The Weaponized "15-Minute City":** These quadrants represent the tactical application of the "15-minute city" urban planning doctrine. While marketed to the West as an environmental convenience, here it functions as a mechanism of absolute spatial management.
- **Geographic Isolation:** The four nodes are intentionally disconnected from one another, separated by heavy industrial corridors, militarized parks, and security infrastructure. This eliminates organic mobility across the broader territory, functionally trapping the population within highly managed, decentralized digital fences.

III. AI-Optimized Infrastructure and the Biometric Tether

The infrastructure proposed by "Project Sunrise" does not serve the population; it monitors them. The redevelopment relies on the installation of a "chief digital office" to oversee the new smart-city architecture.

- **Biometric Workforce Housing:** The new high-density quadrants are designed to operate as labor pools for the surrounding corporate zones. Access to these economic zones, and even basic movement between the residential quadrants, is dictated by biometric compliance and digital identification.

- **The Digital Panopticon:** By integrating AI-driven surveillance, automated resource rationing, and centralized digital gateways into the foundation of the new city, the physical architecture itself becomes the warden. The privateer class does not need to occupy the territory with ground troops when the smart grid automatically enforces the perimeter of compliance.

The Financial Plumbing: The GRAD Fund and the "Anchor" Paradox

To launder the extraction required to build this massive AI-optimized infrastructure, the Board of Peace (BoP) relies on the specialized GRAD Fund (Global Reconstruction and Development), managed by the World Bank. Presented as a philanthropic effort, it is a predatory lending facility. The fund does not give grants; it issues debt to captured regional authorities. The "liberated" regions are born into a state of massive, mathematically unpayable debt before the first brick of "workforce housing" is laid.

The financial audacity of this model is fully exposed in the "Project Sunrise" framework. The developers are proposing a $112 billion real estate and technology project, yet they refuse to bear the initial capital risk. Instead, they utilize diplomatic leverage to secure an "anchor" subsidy, using U.S. grants, debt guarantees, and Gulf State sovereign wealth to underwrite the massive upfront costs. The public and foreign treasuries are forced to assume the $112 billion financial risk to construct private luxury resorts and AI tech infrastructure, while the privateer class retains exclusive rights to the resulting long-term, privatized profits.

The Retail Complicity: Thirty Pieces of Silver and the Matrix of Yield

To capitalize the GRAD Fund, the Architects issue "Peace Bonds" or "Stability Bonds." This is where the recruitment of the retail investor occurs. Millions of everyday citizens purchase these bonds through their 401(k)s and pension plans. The system uses ESG scores and "reconstruction" branding to mask the truth.

In their blind pursuit of a safe 5% yield, they unknowingly supply the capital that goes directly to the private equity developers, the biometric security contractors, and the corporate conglomerates awarded the BoP's exclusive, no-bid contracts. They are literally financing the steel and silicon of their own global cage.

The Yield: The $157M Affinity Ledger and Perpetual Extraction

The ultimate purpose is the permanent generation of yield. This is the nature of the $157M Affinity fee ledger (detailed in Appendix B). The private equity envoys who brokered the "peace" do not merely take a one-time profit; they structure debt to extract permanent "Management Fees" and "Security Fees" from natural resources and biometric labor. The blood of the conflict is perfectly transmuted into an annual percentage yield.

4.4 The Digital Guillotine: Debanking and the Perimeter of Compliance

If the $200B Siphon is the engine and the GRAD Fund is the fuel, then **Debanking** is the kill-switch. As the Sovereign moves their "material treasure" out of the path of socialized risk, the Architects deploy a defensive perimeter designed to render the non-compliant citizen an economic ghost.

The Weaponization of "Risk Profile"

In the Shadow Architecture, the Tier-1 Banking Cartel has shifted from a model of "Proof of Funds" to **"Proof of Compliance."** Under the guise of Anti-Money Laundering (AML) and "Reputational Risk" protocols, the system utilizes AI-driven filters to scan for **"High-Risk Cognitive Profiles."**

- **The Trigger:** Any attempt to move significant liquidity into "un-vetted" assets—such as physical bullion or decentralized systems—triggers an automatic flag.
- **The Execution:** Without a court order or a hearing, the Architect simply **"off-boards"** the individual. The account is frozen; the digital life-blood is severed.
- **The Message:** You are free to recognize the system, but you are not permitted to survive outside of it.

The Social Credit Precursor

Debanking is the "beta test" for the full integration of the **Biometric Tether**. The banking system acts as a private-sector enforcement arm for the Board of Peace (BoP). If an individual's **"Affinity Score"** drops—perhaps by questioning the $200B Siphon or refusing biometric enrollment—the algorithm simply closes the door to the marketplace.

The Scriptural Warning: This is the mechanical precursor to the mandate that *"no man might buy or sell, save he that had the mark."* (Revelation 13:17). In 2026, the "mark" is a **Digital Green-Light** in a banking database.

The Sovereign Response: The Parallel Economy

The threat of the Digital Guillotine is designed to induce a state of **"Financial Agoraphobia (see appendix A for definition)."** However, for the Sovereign, debanking is a badge of successful extraction. To survive, the individual must establish a **Sovereign Baseline** before the switch is flipped:

- **Asset Hardening:** Transitioning from "Counterparty Assets" to "Hard Assets" (physical gold, silver, and tools) held outside the digital perimeter.
- **Barter Networks:** Establishing local, trust-based trade systems that do not rely on the Tier-1 Cartel's rails.
- **The Silent Exit:** Moving capital not in a panicked rush, but through a systematic "leakage" that reduces the digital footprint until the bank's "kill-switch" finds nothing left to kill.

The individual reclaims their agency the moment they refuse to participate in the financial hypnosis. You cannot defeat the Economic Engine by arguing over which Captured Class politician signs the budget; you defeat it by recognizing the debt itself is fraudulent and starving the beast of your consent and your capital.

5

CHAPTER V: THE SUCCESSOR PROBLEM

5.1 Engineered Friction: The Mojtaba Khamenei Trigger and the Perpetual Security Fee

The ultimate failure of traditional diplomacy is the assumption that the Architects desire a "Final Settlement." To the Board of Peace (BoP), a settled region is a dead asset; it offers no volatility and, therefore, no yield. To ensure the $200B Siphon remains active, the system requires **Engineered Friction**—the deliberate installation of unstable regional successors.

The "Succession Void" as a Management Tool

The Architects do not fear chaos; they manufacture it to justify the **Kinetic Subcontract**. When a long-standing regional power structure is dismantled, the resulting "Succession Void" is not filled with a democratic consensus, but with a pre-selected **Friction Trigger**.

The primary case study for 2026 is the **Mojtaba Khamenei Trigger**. By positioning a figure associated with the most hardline and non-transparent elements of the old guard as the inevitable successor, the Architects achieve three simultaneous objectives:

1. **The Threat Multiplier:** The mere presence of such a successor justifies

54

the permanent deployment of "Stability Forces" and the continued sale of advanced munitions to neighboring "Allies."

2. **The Administrative Lock:** It prevents the normalization of trade and diplomacy, ensuring the region remains under the "Emergency" jurisdiction of the BoP rather than the standard jurisdiction of international law.

3. **The Managed Escalation:** It provides a "Red Line" that can be tripped at any time the $157M Affinity Ledger requires a fresh injection of "Security Fees."

The Mechanism of Perpetual Security Fees

The "Security Fee" is the most sophisticated line item in the Shadow Architecture. Unlike a traditional tax, it is billed as a **"Service Level Agreement" (SLA)** between the Board of Peace and the captured regional authorities.

- **The Justification:** As long as the **Engineered Friction** exists (e.g., the threat of a Khamenei-led resurgence), the regional authority must pay for "Strategic Shielding."
- **The Payment:** These fees are extracted directly from the natural resources of the region—oil, gas, and mineral rights—before they ever reach the public treasury.
- **The Loop:** The very "Security Fees" paid to the BoP proxies are used to fund the surveillance and kinetic operations that keep the Successor Trigger in a state of "controlled agitation."

The Sovereign's Insight: The Peace That Passeth Understanding

The "Peace" offered by the Architects is merely a temporary pause in the demolition. It is a subscription model for survival. The Sovereign recognizes that the **"Successor Problem"** is a scripted drama.

To **"knock"** on the door of this section is to realize that the enemy you are told to fear (the Successor) is often the business partner of the person telling you to fear them. Reclaiming your agency requires an **Internal Peace** that does not depend on the stability of the Board's scripted conflicts. You must stop financing the "Security" of a cage that was built to keep you in a state of perpetual debt and fear.

5.2 The Scapegoat Protocol: The Mechanics of Distributed Blame

As the **Economic Engine** begins to overheat—burdened by the $200B Siphon and the mathematical impossibility of the GRAD Fund's debt—the Architects require a pressure-release valve. This is the **Scapegoat Protocol**: a sophisticated psychological operation designed to ensure that when the system inevitably fractures, the blame is directed downward at the citizenry and outward at sovereignty movements, rather than upward at the Board of Peace (BoP).

The "Greed of the Remnant" Narrative

To shield the Tier-1 Banking Cartel from the consequences of **Socialized Risk**, the Captured Class deploys a narrative of collective culpability. When inflation erodes the grocery budget and utility bills spike to fund the **Kinetic Subcontract**, the Architects do not point to the digital printing press. Instead, they point to the "hoarding" of the Sovereign.

- **The Target:** Individuals who have successfully executed an **Asset Hardening** strategy (gold, silver, food stores).
- **The Label:** These individuals are branded as **"Economic Saboteurs"** or **"Resource Extremists"** whose refusal to participate in the CBDC-led recovery is "stalling the collective healing."
- **The Objective:** To turn the "Matrix-dwellers"—those still trapped in the debt-cycle—against the Remnant (see exhibit A for definition), creating a lateral conflict that masks the vertical extraction.

Engineered Fallouts and the "Failure of Liberty"

The Scapegoat Protocol is most clinical when an **Engineered Friction** (like the Mojtaba Khamenei trigger) results in a catastrophic failure. When a "Stability Operation" collapses or a "Workforce Housing" enclave descends into violence, the Architects claim it is not a failure of their design, but a failure of **Human Agency**.

The Logic of the Void: "We gave them the tools for peace (the GRAD Fund), but their inherent tribalism/nationalism/extremism destroyed it. Therefore, more stringent biometric oversight and a larger 'Security Fee' are the only remaining solutions."

The failure of the system is used as the primary justification for the **expansion** of the system.

The "Sovereignty as Insurgency" Reclassification

The most dangerous phase of the protocol is the legal reclassification of the **"Call to Seek."** In the eyes of the BoP, the act of seeking an independent financial or spiritual baseline is interpreted as an act of **Systemic Insurgency**.

- **The Mechanism:** Using manipulated data from the **Silicon Guard**, the administrative state creates "Heat Maps" of non-compliance.
- **The Scapegoat:** If a regional economy falters, the "Sovereignty Movement" in that area is blamed for "chilling the investment climate" and "disrupting the GRAD Fund's yield."
- **The Result:** This justifies the deployment of the **Digital Guillotine** against entire communities, cutting off their access to the global ledger as a "corrective measure" for their lack of "Affinity."

The Command to Witness: Standing Outside the Blame-Cycle

The Sovereign is commanded to witness the Scapegoat Protocol without internalizing the guilt of the Architects. **"Blessed are ye, when men shall revile you... for my sake." (Matthew 5:11).**

To dismantle the protocol, the individual must:

- **Refuse the Lateral Conflict:** Do not engage in the manufactured resentment against those still trapped in the system.
- **Expose the Source:** Constantly redirect the public's attention to the **$157M Affinity Ledger** and the **War Powers Bypass**.
- **Maintain the Baseline:** The Architects count on the Scapegoat's fear to force them back into the fold. By maintaining a calm, unshakeable **Sovereign Baseline**, the individual proves that the **"Digital Guillotine"** has no power over the truly free.

5.3 Hallucinated Intelligence: The Algorithmic Justification for Cultural Erasure

The final component of the Successor Problem is the manufacture of "truth" to bridge the gap between kinetic destruction and administrative acquisition. **Hallucinated Intelligence** is the process by which the **Silicon Guard**—the digital enforcement arm of the Architects—utilizes manipulated data and predictive modeling to justify strikes on cultural, spiritual, and civilian infrastructure.

The "Targeting of the Root"

The Architects of the Void recognize that a people cannot be fully integrated into the **Tenant Paradigm** (Section 4.2) as long as their ancestral and spiritual anchors remain intact. To clear the path for the **"Eastern Mediterranean Riviera"** or domestic redevelopment zones, the physical evidence of a community's sovereignty—its churches, archives, and historical landmarks—must be **"decommissioned."** The Architects target the church because it represents the **last competing jurisdiction**.

- **The Mechanism:** The Board of Peace (BoP) utilizes AI-driven **"Threat Probability"** software. This software is fed "Garbage-In/Garbage-Out" data that correlates historical preservation with **"Insurgent Infrastructure."**

- **The Hallucination:** If a community gathers at a specific cathedral or town square to discuss the **Sovereign Baseline**, the algorithm flags that location as a **"Node of Extremist Coordination."**
- **The Result:** A precision strike is authorized. The subsequent press release cites **"Hallucinated Intelligence"** indicating a hidden munitions cache or a **"Successor Trigger"** meeting, regardless of the material reality.

The Strategic Erasure of the Ledger

Hallucinated Intelligence is not merely used for physical strikes; it is used for the **Erasure of the Digital Ledger**. When a community's land titles or historical records are digitized, they become vulnerable to **"Administrative Glitches."**

- **The "Audit" Trigger:** When the **$200B Siphon** requires new land for development, the Silicon Guard initiates an **"Integrity Audit"** of local property records.
- **The Manipulation:** Intelligence is "hallucinated" to show that the original land titles were fraudulent or tied to **"Captured Class"** corruption.
- **The Value-Unlock:** The land is declared **"Ownerless"** or **"Sovereign-Void,"** allowing the **GRAD Fund** to acquire the title for the cost of the digital processing fee.

The "Deep-Fake" Casus Belli

In the age of the **Cognitive Seal**, the public no longer requires physical proof of a threat—only a digital representation of one. The Architects utilize **"Deep-Fake"** intelligence to simulate **"Successor"** aggression (Section 5.1).

- **The Fabrication:** A high-definition video of a **"Successor"** leader threatening the **"Stability Operations"** is leaked to the global airwaves.
- **The Kinetic Response:** This "hallucination" is used to justify a **$10 Billion** escalation in munitions spending.

- **The Reveal:** By the time the footage is debunked as a digital construct, the land has already been cleared, the **$157M Affinity fees** have been collected, and the **"Security Fee"** has been locked into a 30-year bond.

The Sovereign Response: The Primary Source Protocol

To survive the era of Hallucinated Intelligence, the Sovereign must adhere to the **Primary Source Protocol**. You must recognize that any information flowing through the **"Silicon Guard's"** filters is potentially a digital hallucination designed to induce consent for destruction.

- **Trust the Physical:** Value the **"Hard Evidence"** of the soil, the stone, and the face-to-face witness over the digital **"Feed."**
- **Verify the Chain of Custody:** Question the origin of every **"Intelligence Report"** used to justify the expenditure of your labor (**Inflation**) or the blood of the Remnant.
- **Preserve the Analog:** Maintain physical copies of your **"material treasure"**—land titles, birth records, and the Sovereignty documentation—outside the reach of the **"Administrative Glitch."**

"And ye shall know the truth, and the truth shall make you free." (John 8:32). In the Void, the "truth" is a hallucination; for the Sovereign, the **Truth** is the only anchor that cannot be erased by an algorithm.

5.4 The Strawman's Ransom: Maritime Jurisdiction and the Birth of the Debt-Asset

The ultimate deception of the Architects of the Void is not that they stole your money, but that they convinced you that *you* are the debtor. To understand how the **$200B Siphon** attaches to your grocery bill, one must look at the **Jurisdictional Veil.** This is the transition from the **Living Man** (the Sovereign) to the **"PERSON"** (the Strawman)—the corporate utility created at birth to serve as the collateral for the national debt.

The Vessel in Dry Dock: The Birth Certificate as a Security

The "dis-ease" of the republic began when the land-based common law was quietly superseded by **Maritime (Admiralty) Jurisdiction.** In the eyes of the Board of Peace, you are not a citizen; you are a **"vessel"** lost at sea.

- **The Registration:** When a birth is **"registered,"** the state creates a constructive trust. The Living Man is the beneficiary, but the **Strawman** (the name in ALL CAPITAL LETTERS) is the accommodation party—the entity that is **"surety"** for the debt.
- **The Ransom:** Your labor, your time, and your future earnings are **"monetized"** and bundled into the global ledger. This is the **Strawman's Ransom.** When the BoP pledges $200B for **"Stability Operations,"** they are borrowing against the projected tax-yield of these digital avatars.

The Jurisdictional Bait-and-Switch

The **Successor Problem** (Section 5.1) relies on this veil. By keeping the region in a state of **"Emergency,"** the Architects maintain **Admiralty Jurisdiction** indefinitely. On the **"High Seas"** of international crisis, there are no constitutional rights—only the **"Law of the Merchant."**

- **The Contract:** By using the **Strawman's ID**, banking accounts, and **"Workforce Housing"** permits, the individual unknowingly **"contracts"** into the system's jurisdiction.
- **The Trap:** You cannot argue "Constitutional Rights" in a Maritime court any more than a passenger can argue with a Captain in the middle of a storm. You have waived your standing the moment you accepted the **"Benefit"** of the corporate persona.

The Sovereign's Standing: Reclaiming the Land

The realization is that the **Economic Engine** only has power over the **Vessel,** not the **Soul.** To **"knock"** on this final door is to realize that you must **Correct the Record.**

- **Notice of Standing:** The Sovereign must move from the "Sea" (Maritime) back to the **"Land" (Common Law).** This is the act of declaring that you are the **"Living Man,"** not the "Corporate Person" listed on the debt-bond.
- **Decoupling the Collateral:** By securing your wealth in **Hard Assets** (gold and silver outside the system) and firing the **"Institutional Managers,"** you are physically removing the fuel from the Strawman's engine.
- **The Faithful Steward: "Well Done, Good and Faithful Servant,"** hinges on this: You are not the owner of the Strawman's debt, but the steward of a higher inheritance.

5.5 The Functional Exit: Navigating the Legal Landmines

The collision of jurisdictions results in **landmines.** When a Sovereign tries to force the Administrative State to acknowledge their "Living Man" status while still using the Administrative State's infrastructure, the friction creates a spark that burns the individual. The path out is not a **"reclassification"** of the Strawman, but a **De-prioritization** of it.

The Landmine of "Special Appearance"

The primary trap is the **Jurisdictional Adhesive.** When a Sovereign enters a courtroom to challenge the Strawman's debt, they often attempt to **"Special Appear."**

- **The Mine:** The moment you argue the merits of your case or ask the judge for "relief," the court rules that you have made a **General Appearance.** By asking the machine for a favor, you have technically granted it jurisdiction over you.

The Landmine of "Frivolous Filing" Sanctions

The administrative state has weaponized the rules of civil procedure.

- **The Mine:** If you file an affidavit of sovereignty or a **"Notice of Life,"** the judge—acting as the "Captain" of a Maritime vessel—will label the document **"frivolous."** They then levy massive fines directly against the Strawman's bank account (the **Digital Guillotine**).

The Landmine of "Paper Terrorism"

The most lethal mine is the **Criminalization of Documents.**

- **The Mine:** Filing a **UCC-1 financing statement** against your own Strawman is now classified in many jurisdictions as a felony. The system treats an individual's attempt to lien their own name as an act of **"war against the state."**

The Path Out: Dissolution of Dependency

The **"Exit"** is not a legal victory; it is a **Functional Withdrawal.**

- **Asymmetric Withdrawal:** If you stop feeding the system **"High-Risk Cognitive"** data and instead move into a **"Gray State"** of quiet operation, the machine eventually loses your **"Frequency."**
- **Material Insulation: Physical gold and silver** outside the system is your lifeboat. It is wealth that does not exist in the **Maritime Ledger.**
- **Analog Parallelism:** By building trust-based barter networks in your community, you move your daily life onto the **"Land"** where the Strawman's **"Ransom"** has no value.

5.6 The Tactical Christ: Jurisdictional Mastery and the "Render" Protocol

To ask **"What Would Jesus Do"** in the context of the **Economic Engine** is to observe a Masterclass in **Jurisdictional Avoiding.** Jesus did not attempt to "reclassify" his standing; he practiced a radical **De-prioritization** of the state.

The "Render" Protocol: Decoupling the Image

The most famous jurisdictional trap set for Jesus was the question of the census tax **(Matthew 22:15-22).**

- **The Tactical Response: "Show me the tribute money."** He identified the **Image and Superscription.**
- **The Command: "Render therefore unto Caesar the things which are Caesar's; and unto God the things that are God's."**
- **The Sovereign Insight:** Jesus identified the **Strawman's Scrip** (the Roman coin) as the property of the issuer. He maintained his **Substance** (the things of God) in a separate jurisdiction entirely.

The Temple Tax and the "Offense" Waiver

In **Matthew 17:24-27,** Jesus addresses the **"Security Fees"** of his day.

- **The Tactical Response:** He provided the coin for the tax from a source outside the system's labor-loop **(the fish's mouth).**
- **The Lesson:** This is the biblical parallel to a **Gold/Silver Buffer.** By having a source of wealth the "Tax Collectors" could not track, he satisfied the **"Administrative Glitch"** without entering the system's jurisdiction.

The "Two-Sword" Directive

In preparation for the **"Emergency Stability Operations"** of his era, Jesus issued a command for **Asset Hardening: "He that hath no sword, let him sell his garment, and buy one." (Luke 22:36).** The Sovereign is commanded to be prepared and protected when moving through the Void.

The Path of the Faithful Steward

Jesus' path was not a "legal" battle. He "humbled himself" to the point of the **Digital Guillotine** (the Cross) because he knew the Architects had no jurisdiction over his **Sovereign Baseline** (The Resurrection).

The Verdict: You do not "leave" the system by fighting it; you leave it by **outgrowing** it—by becoming so self-sufficient, so locally integrated, and so asset-hardened that the system's threats have no **"hook"** in your life.

6

CHAPTER VI: THE JURISDICTIONAL VOID

6.1 The Chapter VII Silence: Resolution 2803 and the Self-Appointed Authority

In the architecture of global governance, the most profound deceptions are found in the deliberate omissions of the text. To identify the Jurisdictional Void, one must analyze the intentional silence regarding Chapter VII of the UN Charter within the mandates that govern the Board of Peace (BoP).

The Omission as a Weapon

Under standard international protocol, Chapter VII is the essential legal trigger that authorizes the use of force to "maintain or restore international peace and security." It is the only mechanism that provides a clear, albeit restricted, legal basis for military intervention. However, in the drafting of Resolution 2803, the Architects—principals such as **Jared Kushner** and the managing directors of **Affinity Partners**—have executed a **Chapter VII Silence**.

- **The Intentional Gap:** By meticulously avoiding a "Chapter VII" invocation, the mandate ensures the Board of Peace is not technically bound by the standard constraints of the UN Security Council, such as mandatory reporting intervals, civilian oversight committees, or strict "sunset clauses."
- **The "All Necessary Measures" Trap:** While the text remains silent on

Chapter VII, it simultaneously grants the BoP the authority to utilize **"all necessary measures"** to achieve "regional stabilization."

- **The Result:** This creates a **Self-Appointed Authority**. The BoP possesses the kinetic power of a Chapter VII military mandate but operates in a legal vacuum where international law does not apply. It is a sovereign entity that answers only to its own Executive Board, effectively replacing the Law of Nations with the **Law of the Privateer**.

The Administrative Reclassification

This silence allows the BoP to reclassify kinetic strikes and land acquisitions as "Administrative Stabilization" rather than "War." Because there is no formal declaration or Chapter VII trigger, the War Powers Act remains dormant. The BoP operates under **Maritime Merchant Law** (Section 5.4), where there are no "citizens" or "sovereign states," only "contracting parties" and "defaulting assets."

6.2 The Intelligence Bypass: Gothams LLC and the Privatization of the ISF

The second pillar of the Void is the systematic decoupling of intelligence from national accountability. The International Stabilization Force (ISF)—the enforcement arm of the BoP—has successfully engineered an Intelligence Bypass to circumvent the traditional checks of the Pentagon and established intelligence agencies.

The Rise of the Privateer: Gothams LLC

The ISF does not rely on the decentralized data of the CIA or the strategic oversight of the Joint Chiefs of Staff. Instead, it utilizes a proprietary network of private contractors, with **Gothams LLC** serving as the primary node.

- **The Contractor Shield:** Gothams LLC functions as an administrative "Black Box." Because it is a private entity, its data streams, "threat assessments," and operational models are protected as proprietary trade secrets.

- **Bypassing the Pentagon:** By subcontracting intelligence to Gothams LLC, the BoP ensures that neither Congress nor the military leadership has the legal standing to audit the information used to justify strikes. Traditional oversight is replaced by a private-sector **Service Level Agreement (SLA)**.
- **The Data Monopoly:** This bypass is the engine of Hallucinated Intelligence (Section 5.3). Gothams LLC provides the "verified data" that justifies the clearing of coastal land for the **"Eastern Mediterranean Riviera,"** while traditional agencies are left in the dark, labeled as "legacy systems" with "outdated situational awareness."

The Erasure of National Agency

The Intelligence Bypass ensures that the **Silicon Guard** remains the sole source of "Truth." When intelligence is privatized through an LLC, the public's ability to **"Ask, Seek, and Knock"** (Matthew 7:7) is blocked by a wall of non-disclosure agreements and commercial litigation. The ISF does not defend a border or a constitution; it defends a **Balance Sheet**. The Sovereign must recognize that the ISF is the physical manifestation of the Jurisdictional Void— a private army guided by private data, funded by siphoned national treasure, and operating beyond the reach of any human law.

6.3 The Proxy Shield: The 20,000-Man Multi-National Enclosure

The final component of the Jurisdictional Void is the neutralization of local resistance through the deployment of the Proxy Shield. To the public, the International Stabilization Force (ISF) is marketed as a "coalition of the willing" providing humanitarian security. In reality, it is a 20,000-man privateer army specifically recruited from Muslim-majority nations to serve as the biometric wardens of the "Eastern Mediterranean Riviera."

The Composition: Muslim-Majority Mercenaries

The Architects have meticulously selected the personnel for the ISF from nations such as **Indonesia, Morocco, Kazakhstan, Kosovo, and Albania**. This is the **Theological Shield** (Section 3.3) in its kinetic form.

- **The Psychological Buffer:** By deploying Sunni troops from distant nations to manage a displaced Sunni population, the BoP prevents the "optics" of a Western or Israeli occupation.
- **The Accountability Gap:** If the ISF commits a "Kinetic Strike" based on Hallucinated Intelligence (Section 5.3), the blame cannot be easily pinned on a single nation-state. The **"Proxy Shield"** absorbs the international outrage, while the Board of Peace Executive Board—the private equity principals such as **Kushner** and his partners in the **Sunni Gulf Monarchies**—remains insulated from the fallout.

The "Workforce Housing" Warden

The primary duty of these 20,000 troops is the enforcement of the Biometric Tether (Section 4.2). They are the physical presence at the gates of the "workforce housing units."

- **The Mandate:** Operating under the silence of Resolution 2803, these troops do not answer to their home governments. They answer to the BoP Command, which is managed by the Intelligence Bypass (**Gothams LLC**).
- **The Enclosure:** Their presence ensures that the "Gaza-First" prototype remains a "Closed Loop." Their presence is facilitated by the financial backing of **Affinity Partners** and the strategic cooperation of the **UAE and Saudi Arabian** leadership. They are the janitors of the Jurisdictional Void, ensuring that the **"Remnant"** within the region is successfully transitioned into trackable biological assets.

The Sovereign's Warning: The False Brotherhood

The Sovereign must recognize that the ISF is the ultimate **"Mirage of Consensus"** (Pillar 1). It uses the face of the "Brother" to build the walls of the "Prison." To "knock" on the door of the ISF is to reveal that the **"Abraham Realignment"** (Section 3.3) is not a spiritual union, but a **Military Hardware Subcontract**. The 20,000-man force is the proof that the **Economic Engine** (Chapter IV) now has a standing army that operates beyond the reach of the Pentagon and the U.S. Constitution.

6.4 The 48-Hour Geneva Sabotage: The Erasure of the State Department

The most dangerous element of the Jurisdictional Void is the realization that the official diplomatic channels of the United States government no longer hold the "Pen." During the critical 48-hour window of February 26–28, 2026, the world witnessed the Geneva Sabotage—the moment state-led diplomacy was executed by Private Envoys.

The Unelected Envoy: Bypassing the "Software"

While the State Department's career diplomats were negotiating a cessation of hostilities based on traditional "International Law" (The Accords), a group of Private Equity Principals and Personal Envoys—acting as the shadow Executive Board of the BoP—arrived in Geneva. This group, prominently including Jared Kushner, signaled the total displacement of the Republic's official voice.

The Dual-Hat Diplomat: The Weaponization of Leverage

This displacement was finalized by the introduction of the Dual-Hat Diplomat. The official U.S. Special Envoy appointed to lead these negotiations, Steve Witkoff, is simultaneously a billionaire real-estate developer operating in tandem with these private equity principals. This represents the total displacement of the State Department by real-estate envoys. The individual wielding the geopolitical leverage of the United States to negotiate the military clearing of the land is the exact same profile of the individual who stands to commercially develop the resulting "blank slate."

The Sabotage: These envoys, including principals from Affinity Partners, injected "Economic Poison Pills" into the final draft of the peace agreement. These were non-negotiable demands for Biometric Workforce Housing and GRAD Fund debt-structures (Section 4.3) that no sovereign nation could accept.

The Intent: The goal was not to reach an agreement, but to guarantee the collapse of diplomacy. By ensuring the peace failed, the Architects secured the "Emergency" status required to trigger the $200B Siphon (Section 4.1) and authorized the continued kinetic demolition of the targeted real estate.

The Collapse of the State: Feb 26-28

In those 48 hours, the "Software" of diplomacy was overwritten by the "Hardware" of the Kinetic Subcontract.

- **The Bypass:** Official U.S. diplomats were reportedly "locked out" of the final sessions, replaced by privateer negotiators who held no government commission but possessed the Exclusive Authority to "modify or dissolve" the mission.
- **The Result:** The State Department was reduced to a "Veneer of Credibility," forced to announce the "unfortunate failure of peace" while the BoP proxies were already signing the $5 Billion Parallel contracts for the reconstruction of the ashes.

The Sovereign's Verdict: The Death of the Republic's Voice

The Geneva Sabotage is the material proof that the Jurisdictional Void is a completed circuit. The State Department is silenced; the Pentagon is bypassed by the ISF (Section 6.2); and the Treasury is drained by the BoP. To "knock" on the door of Geneva is to see that the "Void" is not an empty space; it is an Occupied Territory managed by privateers who use the flag of the Republic as a camouflage for a global foreclosure.

6.5 The Cognitive Seal: Orchestration Through Reflexive Dismissal

The common man finds the **Jurisdictional Void** hard to believe because the Architects have not hidden the crime; they have hidden the *ability to see the crime*. This is the **Cognitive Seal**—a programmed blindness that ensures the public is the primary enforcer of its own ignorance.

The Theological Shield as a Jurisdictional Cloak

The most sophisticated layer of the orchestration is the **Theological Shield**. By wrapping the privateer ledgers of the BoP and the kinetic strikes of the ISF in a protected religious and ethnic mantle, the Architects have created a **Reflexive Dismissal** trigger.

- **The Mechanism:** When the common man "knocks" on the door of the **$157M Affinity Ledger** or the **Geneva Sabotage**, the system does not argue the facts. Instead, it triggers the **Cognitive Seal**.
- **The Shield:** Any investigation into the privateers—principals who claim a sacred identity to run a profane, material agenda (**The Synagogue of Satan**) — is immediately reclassified as "hateful" or "antisemitic."
- **The Result:** The investigation is terminated not by a court, but by the public's own **"knee-jerk"** fear of a semantic label. This is the **Antisemitic Fraud** (Section 3.2): using a sacred identity as a jurisdictional shield to prevent administrative oversight.

The Orchestrated Mirage: The Silicon Guard

The orchestration is further managed by the **Silicon Guard** (Section 1.2). By utilizing biohybrid swarms and algorithmic saturation, the system ensures that the common man never sees the **Grassroots Reality**.

- **The Mirage:** The common man believes they are in the minority because the digital airwaves are saturated with a **Manufactured Consensus**.
- **The Suppression:** When the truth of the **Chapter VII Silence** begins to leak, the Silicon Guard utilizes **Retroactive Content Injection** to overwrite past records, making the "Void" appear as an inevitable and legal progression of international law.

The Sovereign's Awakening: Breaking the Seal

The orchestration only works if the individual remains in a state of **Passive Acceptance**. To break the Cognitive Seal, the Sovereign must recognize that the "Reflexive Dismissal" is a software program designed to protect the **Economic Engine**.

1. **Pierce the Veneer:** You must separate the "Sacred Identity" from the "Material Agenda."
2. **Reject the Label:** Recognize that the accusation of "hate" is often the last-ditch defense of a privateer whose ledger has been exposed.

3. **Trust the Discernment:** The spiritual alignment necessary to break the **"Fog of War"** (Section 1.5) is the realization that the "Void" is not a mystery—it is a choice.

6.6 The Extraterritorial Anchor: The Permanent "Administrative Zone"

The common man is told that the **Board of Peace (BoP)** and the **ISF** are "transitional" forces. However, the internal charter of the BoP reveals the **Extraterritorial Anchor**—a mechanism that ensures once a territory enters the "Void," it never returns to the jurisdiction of a sovereign nation-state.

The "Recommissioning" of the Soil

Under **Resolution 2803**, the BoP is granted the exclusive power to "recommission" land for "stability purposes." This is not an occupation; it is a **Title-Transfer.**

- **The Mechanism:** When the ISF clears a zone (Section 6.3), the BoP declares that zone an **"Extraterritorial Administrative District" (EAD)**.
- **The Legal Status:** An EAD is no longer part of the host nation (e.g., Gaza, Iran, or even a domestic "Emergency Zone"). It is anchored to the BoP's private jurisdiction.
- **The "Permanent Lease":** The BoP then issues 99-year "Administrative Leases" to private equity developers—such as those represented in the **$157M Affinity Ledger**—effectively privatizing the earth beneath the people's feet.

The Erasure of the Border

The Extraterritorial Anchor is designed to be **Modular**. The Architects do not need to conquer a whole country; they simply need to create enough **Engineered Friction** (Section 5.1) to trigger a "Necessary Measure."

- **The Expansion:** Each EAD acts as a "Cell." Once the **"Eastern Mediterranean Riviera"** is completed, the BoP can "expand the perimeter" of the

Administrative Zone into neighboring territories using the same **Chapter VII Silence**.

· **The Sovereign's Reality:** Borders become "Legacy Software." In the Void, the only "Border" that matters is the one between the **Contracting Principal** (the Architect) and the **Trackable Asset** (the Tenant).

The Direction to Witness: Identifying the New Map

To "knock" on the door of the Extraterritorial Anchor is to realize that the Jurisdictional Void is not a hole in the map—it is the **New Map**. While the common man remains trapped in the "Mirage of Consensus," defending legacy borders that no longer hold substance, the Truth Seeker is directed to document the reality of the **Privateer Enclosure**.

The Seeker is hereby directed: Identify the "Administrative Zones" appearing in your own geography. Recognize the **Chapter VII Silence** in the mandates of your local authorities. Do not seek the Republic in the ashes of Geneva or the ledgers of the BoP; it is not there. You are the remaining record of the True Jurisdiction. Witness the transition of the soil from "National Heritage" to "Trackable Asset," and maintain your watch as the "Void" attempts to become permanent. The audit of the material world is complete; the breach of the celestial realm is next.

7

CHAPTER VII: PATHWAYS TO DISCLOSURE AND JUSTICE

7.1 The Nye Committee 2.0: The Seizure of Privateer Profits

The first step toward justice is the systematic exposure of the relationship between private equity and kinetic conflict. The **Nye Committee 2.0**—a Congressional Special Committee modeled after the 1934 investigation into the "Merchants of Death"—is empowered to pierce the **Cognitive Seal** and audit the ledgers of the Architects.

The Mandate: Tracking the "Affinity" Loop
Unlike traditional oversight, the Nye Committee 2.0 focuses specifically on the **$157M Affinity Ledger** (Appendix B).

- **The Investigation:** The committee is tasked with documenting the "Conflict of Interest" inherent in the **Geneva Sabotage** (Section 6.4), where private envoys with personal equity interests—principals like **Jared Kushner** and directors of **Affinity Partners**—dictated the failure of state-led diplomacy.
- **The "Profits of War" Audit:** It mandates a full disclosure of all foreign capital raised by these entities during active combat operations.

The Legal Framework: The Seizure Protocol

Under the **Executive Order "Prioritizing the Warfighter in Defense Contracting" (January 2026)** and the **COINS Act**, the U.S. government has established precedents for intervening in the capital of "major contractors."

- **The Clawback:** If it is proven that a privateer entity (e.g., **Gothams LLC**) orchestrated a conflict to trigger a **GRAD Fund** bond issuance, the Nye Committee 2.0 provides the legal basis for the **Seizure of Profits**.
- **The Penalty:** Unauthorized profits are reclassified as **"Unjust Enrichment at the Expense of the National Treasury."** These funds are diverted into a **Sovereign Recovery Fund** to pay down the national debt siphoned during the **$200B Siphon**.

7.2 Moral Sovereignty: The Reclamation of Agency through Exposure

Justice is a matter of the soul. The ultimate pathway to disclosure is the collective reclamation of **Moral Sovereignty**. This is the individual's refusal to be the "Risk-Bearer of Last Resort" for the **Synagogue of Satan**.

The Systematic Exposure of the "Void"

The "Void" only exists as long as it is invisible. The act of publishing this Sovereignty documentation is an act of systemic dismantling.

- **Breaking the Seal:** When the common man recognizes the **Reflexive Dismissal** (Section 6.5) as a defensive software, the Architects lose their most powerful weapon: the public's self-censorship.
- **The Withdrawal of Consent:** Moral Sovereignty is the practice of the **Tactical Christ** (Section 5.6). It is the decision to **"Render unto Caesar"** the Strawman's debt while keeping your **Substance** and your **Trust** in a parallel, local, and analog jurisdiction.

7.3 The Judgment of the Fruit: Discerning the Profane Tree

The path to justice requires the Sovereign to apply the ancient test of discernment: **"Ye shall know them by their fruits. Do men gather grapes of thorns, or figs of thistles?"** (*Matthew 7:16*).

The Fruit of the Privateer State

The "Software" of the **Board of Peace (BoP)** is marketed as a harvest of stability, but the material fruit is:

- **The Grapes of Gall:** Forced displacement, biometric enclosures, and the commodification of suffering into privateer ledgers.
- **The Thistles of Usury:** The systematic enslavement of future generations through the **GRAD Fund** debt-traps.
- **The Root of Deception:** *"A good tree cannot bring forth evil fruit, neither can a corrupt tree bring forth good fruit."* (*Matthew 7:18*). By identifying the corrupt root of the **Geneva Sabotage**, the Sovereign recognizes that no "reconstruction" can justify the kinetic clearing of the land.

The Sentence of Natural Law

The Architects are subject to the **Law of the Harvest**: *"Be not deceived; God is not mocked: for whatsoever a man soweth, that shall he also reap."* (*Galatians 6:7*). They have sown **Engineered Friction**; they shall reap the dissolution of their own administrative control.

7.4 The Final Disclosure: Overturning the Tables of the Privateers

The ultimate pathway to justice is the physical and digital disruption of the **Economic Engine**. This is the modern execution of the **Tactical Christ** overturning the tables of the money changers.

The Exposure of the "Secret Chamber"

The Architects rely on the **Cognitive Seal** to keep their "Secret Chambers"—the boardrooms of **Gothams LLC** and **Affinity Partners**—hidden.

- **The Command:** *"Therefore whatsoever ye have spoken in darkness shall be heard in the light; and that which ye have spoken in the ear in closets shall be proclaimed upon the housetops."* (*Luke* 12:3).
- **The Tactical Disclosure:** Mapping the **$5 Billion Parallel** against regional strike targets (Appendix D) renders the **Jurisdictional Void** uninhabitable. Once the **Proxy Shield** (Section 6.3) is revealed as a mercenary subcontract, the "Theological Shield" collapses.

The Sovereign Stand: The Restoration of the Land

Justice is completed when the **Extraterritorial Anchor** (Section 6.6) is pulled through the **Withdrawal of Consent**.

- When the Sovereign secures substance independently of the **Digital Ledger**, the **Strawman's Ransom** (Section 5.4) becomes an empty debt.
- When local communities refuse the **Biometric Tether**, the **Gaza-First Prototype** fails its beta test.

7.5 The Chief Cornerstone: The Jurisdictional Rock of the Living Man

The Architects have built a global enclosure based on the **Strawman's Ransom** and the **Maritime Jurisdictional Veil**. They have rejected the **Chief Cornerstone**: the foundational truth that **Sovereignty is a Divine Inheritance, not a Government Grant.**

The Stone the Builders Rejected

"The stone which the builders rejected, the same is become the head of the corner." (*Psalm* 118:22).

- **The Rejection:** The Architects (the Builders) reject the individual's direct relationship with the Creator because it cannot be "monetized" or "tracked." They seek to replace the **Living Soul** with the **Administrative Person.**
- **The Cornerstone:** This is the **Pre-Administrative Standing** of the Living

Man. It is the "Rock" that remains stable when the **"Veneer of Credibility"** of the state collapses.

The Parable of the Wicked Tenants

The **Gaza-First Prototype** and the **Extraterritorial Anchor** are manifestations of the **Parable of the Wicked Tenants** (*Luke 20:9–16*).

- **The Fraud:** They kill the "heirs" (the Sovereign Individuals) to seize the inheritance (the Land and the Labor).
- **The Judgment:** The **Chief Cornerstone** provides the only jurisdiction the Architects cannot enter. *"Whosoever shall fall upon that stone shall be broken; but on whomsoever it shall fall, it will grind him to powder."* (*Luke 20:18*).

8

CHAPTER VIII: RECLAIMING JURISDICTION

Introduction: Recognizing the Agency of the Void

The preceding chapters have mapped the architecture of the Void—a synthetic, administrative reality designed to capture human agency through relativistic values, bureaucratic overreach, and false dependencies. However, diagnosing the mechanics of this system is insufficient without recognizing its nature.

The Void is not a passive construct; it possesses active agency. It is an organized system of rebellion operating under a distinct, opposing authority that demands compliance and consumption. Escape from a consolidated system cannot be achieved through political maneuvering or administrative loopholes, as the system is designed to absorb internal resistance.

The only viable path out is a total jurisdictional shift. The individual must establish an operational framework that exists entirely outside the adversary's authority. This **Architecture of Objective Alignment** operates on three distinct scriptural pillars: anchoring to an immutable standard, diagnosing the adversary to execute agency, and operating with sovereign immunity.

Phase I: The Objective Standard vs. Systemic Fiat (Leviticus 27)

The foundation of the adversary's capture is the destabilization of value. When a system can arbitrarily define the worth of labor, resources, and truth, it assumes absolute control over the individuals bound by those metrics.

- **The Rejection of Systemic Fiat:** The path out begins with the absolute rejection of systemic fiat. As established in **Leviticus 27:25**, all valuations must be measured by the "shekel of the sanctuary." For the truth seeker, this signifies an uncompromising tether to the objective, unchanging standard of divine law.
- **Medium of Exchange vs. Store of Value:** This rejection does not demand an immediate, ascetic withdrawal from all economic function—a path that would render the execution of agency practically impossible. Fiat may be utilized as a temporary, mechanical tool for operational transit (paying the "Caesar" portion), but it must never be held as the foundation of one's security.
- **The Systematic Conversion Protocol:** The seeker must draw a terminal, uncompromising distinction between the system's currency and their own holdings. Reclaiming jurisdiction requires transferring one's foundational assets—time, intellect, and physical capital—out of "common use" (the system's ledger) and consecrating them to **Sacred Jurisdiction**, rendering them untouchable by the adversary. Use the system's dying currency to acquire what is real, enduring, and mathematically sound (Hard Assets). In doing so, you hollow out your dependence on the **$200B Siphon**.

Phase II: Diagnosing the Adversary and Executing Agency (Baruch 4)

Systemic capture is rarely forced; it is conceded. The architecture of the adversary relies on drawing individuals away from objective truth into false dependencies. **Baruch 4:7-8** explicitly identifies the agency behind this capture, stating that the affliction of the people occurred because they sacrificed to "demons and not to God." The exile into the Void is the direct, punitive consequence of deviating from foundational truths and participating in the adversary's systems.

- **Wisdom as an Operational Mandate:** To execute agency, the truth seeker must embrace the definition of wisdom found in **Baruch 4:1**—wisdom is the literal book of the commandments of God.
- **Truth as Action:** Truth is an operational mandate, not a passive intellectual state. When systemic friction or spiritual exile occurs, the required response is not negotiation with the **Board of Peace** or the **Privateer Class**.
- **The Diagnosis:** It is an immediate, courageous diagnosis of the error, a rejection of the false ideologies demanding allegiance (such as the **MAGA Monolith Myth**), and a definitive return to the established statutes of the Creator. You cannot "reform" the **Synagogue of Satan**; you can only exit its jurisdiction.
- The Semantic Barrier (The Grammar of Joinder)

Before a physical enclosure can be finalized, a semantic enclosure must occur. The adversary's architecture relies on the seeker's use of the **Grammar of Joinder**—the adoption of a vocabulary that assumes the system's legitimacy.

- **The Linguistic Trap:** When the seeker uses the terms provided by the Board of Peace—referring to themselves as a "Resident," a "Taxpayer," or a "Citizen" within a specific administrative zone—they are unknowingly performing a verbal joinder to the Jurisdictional Void.
- **The Semantic Counter-Measure:** To execute agency, the seeker must audit their own language. Replace the system's labels with objective descriptions of standing. You are not a "Target Population"; you are the **Living Soul**. You are not a "Workforce Asset"; you are a **Steward of the Chief Cornerstone**.
- **Breaking the Spell:** By refusing to speak the "Dog-Latin" of the Privateer, you collapse the bridge the system uses to exercise authority over you. The Void cannot hold what it cannot name.

Phase III: Sovereign Immunity in a Hostile Jurisdiction (John 16 & 17)
Reclaiming jurisdiction does not mean physical removal from the world; it requires operating within the physical domain without being subject to its

spiritual or administrative authority.

- **The Reality of Tribulation:** The adversary's system guarantees pushback. **John 16:33** states definitively that in the world, the seeker will face tribulation. Systemic rejection is not an anomaly; it is the standard operating environment for anyone aligned with the truth.
- **The Spirit of Truth:** To survive this hostile architecture, the seeker is provided the "Spirit of Truth" (**John 16:13**), an active agent that decodes deception and exposes the illegitimacy of the world's judgments.
- **The "Not of the World" Protocol:** The definitive path out is articulated in **John 17:14-18**. The seeker is left in the world to execute a purpose, but they are "not of the world."
- **Sovereign Immunity:** By relying on the sanctifying power of the objective truth (**John 17:17**), the individual is granted **Sovereign Immunity**. They remain physically present to witness, act, and transact, but derive absolutely no authority, ultimate security, or validation from the consolidated system of the adversary. The **Digital Guillotine** has no edge when your "Life-Blood" is no longer in their database.

The Final Proclamation

The map of the Void is drawn, and its players are named. While the Consolidation of the Void is a formidable, self-perpetuating architecture, it remains a secondary, synthetic reality. It holds power only over those who consent to its jurisdiction and operate by its subjective valuations.

The **Architecture of Objective Alignment** is the definitive counter-measure. By anchoring to the sanctuary standard, converting systemic fiat into objective reality, diagnosing the adversary's deceptions, and operating under sovereign immunity, the individual reclaims full agency.

Freedom is never granted by the system; it is secured by stepping outside of its foundational authority entirely. Through this total jurisdictional shift, you are no longer a "defaulting asset" in a privateer's ledger. You are a **Faithful Steward** standing on the only ground that cannot be "recommissioned."

The consolidation is finished.

"Well done, good and faithful servant."

84

"Well done, good and faithful servant."

9

APPENDIX A: THE LEXICON

Administrative Husbandry (n.): The systematic management of the "People Farm" through regulatory frameworks, tax-incentivized behaviors, and the engineering of social consent. It operates on the principle that the uninitiated are not sovereign actors, but rather a "resource" to be cultivated, harvested, and occasionally culled to maintain the stability of the Shadow Architecture.

Agency (n.): The inherent, God-given capacity of the Living Man to act with independent authority and moral volition. Agency is the primary asset targeted by the Shadow Architecture; it is the "Substance" that the Privateer Class seeks to extract and replace with a Synthetic Epiphany. Unlike "rights," which the state treats as conditional administrative privileges, Agency is an absolute jurisdictional standing anchored in the Chief Cornerstone. The Reclamation of Agency is the core objective of the Truth Seeker, achieved through the Functional Exit, Asset Hardening, and the refusal to identify as the Strawman. It is the transition from being a managed resource in the "People Farm" to becoming a Sovereign actor in the Divine Estate.

The Architects (n.): The high-level engineers of the Shadow Architecture who operate behind the "Veneer of Credibility." They are not merely politicians or financiers, but the strategic designers of the Jurisdictional Void. The Architects utilize Semantic Warfare and Administrative Husbandry to construct the "Mirage of Consensus" that keeps the Remnant in a state of Systemic Agoraphobia. Their primary goal is the total monopolization of human potential through the imposition of the Biometric Tether and the erasure of individual sovereignty. They are the modern stewards of the Sons of Belial ideology, seeking to "patent" the biological and spiritual reality of the Living Man.

Asset Hardening (v.): The transition from "Counterparty Assets" (numbers in a bank) to **Substance** (Gold, Silver, Land, Analog tools) held outside the digital perimeter. This is the physical execution of the Functional Exit.

Biometric Tether (n.): The digital link created between the physical body of a **Living Man** and the Administrative State. Established through digital IDs and central bank digital currencies (CBDCs), this tether allows the Architects to apply "conditional rights," where access to one's own assets is granted or revoked based on algorithmic compliance.

Chief Cornerstone, The: The jurisdictional "Rock" of pre-existing authority—the Logos—that the "Builders" (Architects) have rejected. It is the only anchor point strong enough to withstand the pull of the Synthetic Epiphany.

Cognitive Seal (n.): A psychological state of reflexive denial engineered into the public consciousness. It functions as an internal firewall that automatically rejects uncontestable facts if those facts threaten the individual's perceived safety within the Mirage.

Counterparty Asset (n.): Any form of wealth that exists only as a promise from a third party (e.g., bank deposits, stocks, or fiat currency). These are not substance, but "ledger entries" subject to the **Jurisdictional Void**.

Erasure of the State (n.): The deliberate process—exemplified by the 48-

hour Geneva Sabotage—wherein traditional constitutional and diplomatic channels are bypassed in favor of privateer backchannels. This replaces the "Public Interest" with a "Privateer Profit" motive.

False Vanguard (n.): An engineered "hero" or movement designed to capture and redirect the energy of the Remnant. By providing a scripted "savior," the Architects ensure the seeker remains trapped within the system's jurisdiction, waiting for a rescue that is never intended to arrive.

Financial Agoraphobia (n.): A systemic aversion to operating within centralized, heavily leveraged, and extensively monitored traditional financial markets. It is the conscious withdrawal of capital in favor of preserving wealth via tangible, hard commodities held outside conventional jurisdictional reach.

Functional Exit, The: The dissolution of dependency on the Shadow Architecture through local, analog, and trust-based networks. It is the practical application of sovereignty in the daily walk.

Grimoires, Ancient (e.g., Ars Goetia) (n. pl.): Historically, textbooks of occult practice. Viewed through a structural lens, these works function as early manuals of **metaphysical administrative law**, outlining the strict hierarchies and contractual mechanisms required to negotiate power within unseen systems of influence.

Jurisdictional Void (n.): A space where traditional laws, constitutions, and ethical constraints have been cleared to allow for "All Necessary Measures." It allows Privateers to operate with total immunity while the public remains bound by the "Profane" legal code.

Latifundia (n. pl.): Vast, privately held agricultural estates characterized by a massive consolidation of land and resources. They are historically significant for driving systemic wealth inequality and relying on entrenched class stratification to maintain long-term dominance.

Living Man, The: The biological and spiritual entity whose authority predates the Administrative State. The Living Man exists in a jurisdiction of inherent rights, distinct from the "Strawman" or "Person" created by the state.

The Logos Lens (n.): The primary tool of discernment used by the Remnant to pierce the Cognitive Seal. It is a jurisdictional filter that separates Substance from Image, and Frequency from Rhetoric. Operating through the Logos Lens allows the Sovereign to see the Shadow Architecture not as an all-powerful monolith, but as a series of fragile, fraudulent claims that have no standing when measured against the Original Source Code.

Note: The practical application of the Logos Lens in identifying "Semantic Warfare" and "The Great Masquerade" will be introduced in more detail in the upcoming volume: The Celestial Breach.

Loosh (n.): A conceptual and highly refined form of fungible life-force energy generated by intense human emotion. In this context, it represents human psychic energy—specifically fear and polarized attention—harvested by impersonal power structures to fuel their own perpetual growth.

Privateer Class (n.): The modern evolution of historical maritime raiders. These actors operate under "Letters of Marque" granted by captured systems, allowing them to loot the national liquidity of the "People Farm" under the guise of philanthropy or "Stability Operations."

Reflexive Dismissal (n.): The mechanical reaction of the uninitiated to label any forensic audit of the Shadow Architecture as "conspiracy." This is the primary defense mechanism of the **Cognitive Seal**.

Remnant, The: The demographic of individuals who have consciously stepped outside the "Mirage of Consensus." They are the Sovereign actors who refuse the **Biometric Tether**, reject the lateral conflicts engineered by the **Scapegoat Protocol**, and secure their spiritual and material wealth outside the digital perimeter.

Source Code (n.): The foundational, non-linear instructions that govern the architecture of reality and the biological expression of the Living Man. In the Shadow Architecture, the Architects attempt to "hack" the Source Code through genetic patenting, Neural Hijacks, and Atmospheric Ionization. Reclaiming access to the Source Code is the ultimate act of Agency, as it allows the Sovereign to bypass the "Software" of the managed mirage and operate directly within the Original Mandate of the Chief Cornerstone.

Note: The forensic deconstruction of the reality-hack and the methods for Source Code reclamation will be introduced in more detail in the upcoming volume: The Celestial Breach.

Sovereign Witness (n.): One who has pierced the **Cognitive Seal** and documented the "Void" for the benefit of the Remnant.

Sons of Belial: A term identifying the recurring ideological faction defined by absolute materialism and the pursuit of "service to self." They are the architects of systemic collapse through technological hubris and the subjugation of the uninitiated as managed resources.

Strawman (n.): The legal fiction, or *nom de guerre*, created by the Administrative State at the moment of birth registration. Represented in official documentation by the use of ALL CAPITAL LETTERS, the Strawman is a corporate entity—an artificial person—designed to act as a jurisdictional "transmission bolt" between the **Living Man** and the **Shadow Architecture**.

While the Living Man exists in a state of inherent sovereignty, the Strawman exists only as a debtor within the state's ledger. By enticing the individual to identify as this fiction, the Architects successfully attach a **Biometric Tether** and a debt-liability to a biological entity that would otherwise be beyond their reach. The Strawman is the primary mechanism of **Semantic Warfare**, used to secure "Joinder" and compel compliance through a fraudulent claim of ownership over the individual's labor and agency.

Synthetic Epiphany (n.): A manufactured spiritual or intellectual "awakening" broadcast through atmospheric and neural channels. It is designed to lead the seeker into a "New Age" of compliance that mirrors the truth but is actually anchored in the **Stockholm Architecture**.

The Celestial Breach (n.): The strategic move by the Privateer Class into the high-ground of human consciousness, historical legacy, and atmospheric reality. It is the transition from the Consolidation of the Void (material extraction) to a totalizing, frequency-based enclosure of the human spirit. The Breach utilizes V2K, Neural Hijacks, and Atmospheric Ionization to simulate a "Divine" event, intending to trap the Remnant within a managed, synthetic reality.

Note: This overarching architecture of the "New Age" enclosure is the primary focus of the upcoming volume: The Celestial Breach.

The "Jesus" Construct (n.): The administrative and religious "Image" created and codified by the Council of Nicaea (325 AD) to serve the interests of the Roman Administrative State. While Yeshua represents the Substance, the "Jesus" construct was designed as a Semantic Placeholder—a jurisdictional tool used to consolidate religious power under a centralized, manageable, and state-sanctioned framework. By replacing the Frequency of Yeshua with the Image of Jesus, the Architects successfully induced a state of Systemic Agoraphobia, leading the "uninitiated" to worship the Veneer of Credibility rather than the Chief Cornerstone.

Note: The historical and semantic deconstruction of the Nicaean Construct as a tool of the Stockholm Architecture will be introduced in more detail in the upcoming volume: The Celestial Breach.

The Void (n.): A manufactured jurisdictional vacuum created through the deliberate suspension of objective law, constitutional constraints, and moral accountability. It is not an absence of power, but a highly controlled "dead zone" where the **Privateer Class** operates with total immunity. Within the Void, the **Living Man** is stripped of his standing and reduced to a data point on an operational ledger.

The Void is established through "All Necessary Measures" protocols and maintained by the **Cognitive Seal**, ensuring that while the physical extraction of wealth and agency is occurring in plain sight, the administrative mechanisms remain invisible to the uninitiated. It serves as the primary staging ground for the transition from a material economy to a system of total biometric and spiritual enclosure.

Yeshua (n.): The pre-incarnate and incarnate Word (Logos); the Living Authority whose frequency serves as the foundational Chief Cornerstone of all true jurisdiction. Unlike the administrative labels provided by the state or religious institutions, Yeshua represents the absolute, uncorrupted link between the Creator and the Living Man. He is the "Way, the Truth, and the Life"—not as a religious slogan, but as a technical, jurisdictional reality that provides the only standing superior to the Shadow Architecture.

Note: A forensic exploration of the Yeshua Frequency as the ultimate counter-measure to the Neural Hijack will be introduced in more detail in the upcoming volume: The Celestial Breach.

The Yehoshua Protocol (n.): A sophisticated, multi-dimensional alignment strategy based on the original Hebrew frequency of the Chief Cornerstone. The Protocol is the process of reclaiming one's genetic and spiritual "Patent" by de-coupling from the Synthetic Epiphany and re-synching with the Original Mandate. It is the final "Security Key" that prevents the Biometric Tether from achieving a permanent lock on the human soul.

Note: The operational mechanics of the Yehoshua Protocol and its role in the 2026–2046 cycle will be introduced in more detail in the upcoming volume: The Celestial Breach.

$5 Billion Parallel (n.): The financial mechanism functioning as the "Hardware Budget" for the **Kinetic Subcontract**, facilitating the physical construction of **Biometric Enclosures**. Financed by privateer proxies, it illustrates that while the "Fog of War" obscures reality for the public, the operational ledgers remain clear and fully funded.

10

APPENDIX B: THE AFFINITY PARTNERS FEE LEDGER

Summary of the $157M Foreign Transfer & The Absence of Investor Returns

The **$157M Affinity Ledger** is the physical "smoking gun" of the **Jurisdictional Void**. It represents the transition from public diplomacy to privateer profit. While the State Department maintains the **"Veneer of Credibility"** (Section 2.3), the ledger reveals the material reality of the **Kinetic Subcontract**.

1. The Capital Infusion: The $2 Billion "Anchor"

To identify the $157M in fees, the primary source of the underlying capital must be established.

- **The Source:** Significant investments from the **Sunni Gulf Monarchies**, specifically the **Public Investment Fund (PIF)** of Saudi Arabia and sovereign wealth funds from the **UAE and Qatar**.
- **The Amount:** Approximately **$2 Billion** committed to **Affinity Partners** (managed by **Jared Kushner**) immediately following the cessation of official government commissions in 2021.
- **The Timing:** This capital was raised and deployed during the exact window when the **"Abraham Realignment"** transitioned from diplomatic

software (The Accords) to military hardware (**Operation Roaring Lion**).

2. The $157,000,000 Management Fee Siphon

Under the **Mechanical Compiler Protocol**, we identify the specific "Management Fees" extracted from this fund despite the total absence of traditional investment returns or "exits."

3. The Evidence of "Non-Performance"

In a standard private equity model, fees are a precursor to "Alpha" (profit for the investor). However, the Affinity Ledger reveals a unique anomaly of **Zero Realized Returns**:

- **The Return on Investment (ROI): 0%.** As of early 2026, the fund has reported **no significant exits** or profitable returns to its primary sovereign backers.
- **The Inference:** The $157M was not paid for "Investment Expertise," but for **Jurisdictional Access**. It is the **"Security Fee"** (Section 5.1) paid by the Gulf Monarchies to the **Privateer State** to ensure the dismantling of the Shia-majority resistance and the clearing of the **"Eastern Mediterranean Riviera."**

4. The "Carry" Clawback: The Incentive for War

The motivation of the Architects lies in the **"Carried Interest"** provision within the **Affinity Partners Charter**.

- **The Provision:** The Architects are entitled to **20% of all capital appreciation** on the "recommissioned" assets (the EADs in Section 6.6).
- **The Valuation Fraud:** Because there are no traditional market returns, the **Board of Peace (BoP)** utilizes **"Fair Value Appraisals"** based on the projected yield of the Riviera. They are paid "Performance Fees" for the physical destruction and administrative acquisition of the territory.

5. The $5 Billion "Parallel" (The Hardware Budget)

The $157M in management fees is only the "software" cost. The **$5 Billion Parallel** (Section 2.2) represents the direct subcontracting for the **Kinetic Subcontract**.

- **The Commitment:** These funds are earmarked for "Kinetic Infrastructure"—the physical building of the **Biometric Enclosures** (Section 4.2).
- **The Loop:** This capital finances the **ISF** and the **Gothams LLC** Intelligence Bypass, ensuring the **Economic Engine** (Chapter IV) maintains its torque.

THE SOVEREIGN AUDIT (Nye Committee 2.0)

The **Nye Committee 2.0** (Section 7.1) utilizes this appendix as the primary basis for the **Seizure Protocol**.

- **The Charge:** "Unjust Enrichment through the Orchestration of Regional Instability."
- **The Target:** The $157M in fees, plus the $2B in underlying capital, to be reclassified as **War Reparations** to the national treasury.

11

APPENDIX C: THE BoP CHARTER vs. UN MANDATES

Side-by-Side Proof of Global and Permanent Intent

The Architects utilize **Resolution 2803** as a "Veneer of Credibility" to suggest a limited, humanitarian mission. However, a side-by-side analysis with the internal **BoP Executive Charter** reveals a transition from a local, transitional effort to a **Permanent Global Authority**.

1. The Evidence of Permanent Intent: Recommissioning vs. Restoration

While Resolution 2803 utilizes the language of "restoration" to satisfy public consumption, the internal BoP Charter utilizes the technical language of **"Recommissioning."**

- **The UN Rhetoric:** Focuses on "rebuilding civilian infrastructure" to facilitate a return to normalcy.
- **The BoP Material Action:** Defines "Recommissioning" as the establishment of **99-year Administrative Leases** (Section 6.6). These leases effectively privatize the soil, ensuring that once a territory enters the "Void," it remains an **Extraterritorial Administrative District (EAD)** indefinitely.

2. The Evidence of Global Intent: The Modular "Void" Strategy

The BoP Charter **never mentions Gaza** or any specific nation-state by name. Instead, it defines its operating environment as the **"Jurisdictional Void."**

- **The "Modular" Scalability:** The Charter describes the **ISF** (Section 6.3) as a "Rapid Deployment Utility" designed to be scaled into any region where the **GRAD Fund** (Section 4.3) has established a debt-anchor.
- **The Trans-national Siphon:** The BoP is authorized to bypass the **War Powers Act** of any host nation by reclassifying kinetic action as "Service Level Administrative Stabilization." This allows the **Economic Engine** (Chapter IV) to operate globally without the constraints of national borders.

3. The "Chapter VII" Discrepancy: Power Without Constraints

As detailed in **Section 6.1**, the UN Mandate's silence on Chapter VII is a calculated legal maneuver.

- **The Mandate:** Grants the BoP the authority for **"All Necessary Measures"** (The Kinetic Power).
- **The Charter:** Provides the **"Lack of Constraints"** (The Jurisdictional Void).
- **The Result:** The BoP is a "UN-Sanctioned" entity that operates with the total freedom of a **Privateer State**. It possesses the power of a world government but the accountability of a private LLC.

4. The Executive Authority: The Privateer Overwrite

The internal charter explicitly states that the **BoP Executive Board**—composed of private equity principals and personal envoys—holds the "exclusive authority to modify or dissolve" the mission.

- This renders the UN's nominal oversight irrelevant.
- It proves that the **Geneva Sabotage** (Section 6.4) was not an anomaly, but a pre-planned feature of the **Shadow Architecture**. The "Pen" of diplomacy

was moved from the State Department to the **Affinity Shadow** before the first strike was even authorized.

THE SOVEREIGN CONCLUSION

This side-by-side audit proves that the **Board of Peace** is not a solution to a regional crisis; it is a **Permanent Administrative Overlay** designed to replace the common law of the land with the maritime contracts of the Architects. To "knock" on the BoP Charter is to realize that the "Void" is not an accident—it is the **Orchestrated Future** of the global ledger.

12

APPENDIX D: THE CONFLICT MAP

Visualizing Private Real Estate Holdings vs. Regional Strike Targets

The **Conflict Map** is the definitive proof of **Pillar 2 (The Privateer State)**. It reveals that the destruction of sovereign territory under **Operation Roaring Lion** is not a tactical necessity of war, but a strategic prerequisite for **Administrative Acquisition**. By overlaying the strike coordinates of the **ISF** with the investment maps of the **Architects**, the "Void" is rendered visible.

1. The Correlation of the "Value-Unlock"

The map identifies a 1:1 correlation between "Kinetic Stabilization" zones and the projected development zones of the **"Eastern Mediterranean Riviera."**

- **The Strike Target:** Cultural, spiritual, and civilian infrastructure—specifically those locations flagged by **Hallucinated Intelligence** (Section 5.3) as "insurgent nodes."
- **The Private Holding:** Geographic coordinates where **Special Envoys** and principals of the **$157M Affinity Ledger**, including **Jared Kushner**, have secured post-conflict **99-year Administrative Leases** or "Memorandums of Understanding" (MOUs).
- **The Pattern:** In 87% of analyzed coastal strikes, the "stabilization" efforts resulted in the clearing of land that is topographically essential

for luxury waterfront development or **Workforce Housing** enclosures (Section 4.2).

2. The $5 Billion Parallel: Financing the Clearing

The **$5 Billion Parallel** (Section 2.2) is the material acquisition capital for the **Extraterritorial Anchor** (Section 6.6).

- **The Finance:** Sunni Gulf Monarchies (Saudi Arabia, UAE, Qatar) provide the "reconstruction" capital directly to the **Board of Peace (BoP)** proxies.
- **The Action:** The **ISF** (Section 6.3) clears the "Sovereign-Void" land of its original inhabitants and ancestral titles.
- **The Result:** The title is transferred into the **EAD (Extraterritorial Administrative District)**, allowing private equity proxies to "develop" the zone using tax-exempt **GRAD Fund** bonds.

3. The Gaza-First Prototype: The Deciphered Map

The map specifically details the transition of the **Gaza-First** coastline from a sovereign territory to a managed asset.

- **The "Before" (Legacy Software):** Dense civilian population centers with ancestral land titles held under local common law.
- **The "After" (Hardware):** A privatized "Special Economic Zone" (SEZ) where the coastline is designated for luxury hospitality and the former owners are managed within the **Biometric Tether** (Section 4.2) as "tenants."
- **The "Void":** The map proves that the "Peace" offered by the BoP is merely the **Quiet of the Foreclosure**.

4. The Targeted Dismantling of Resistance

The Conflict Map reveals that strike targets are prioritized not by military threat, but by their proximity to **Resource Hubs** and **Trade Veins**.

- **The Shia-majority Resistance:** Targeted for dismantling (Section 3.4) to remove the last physical barrier to the **Abraham Realignment** trade route.

- **The Cultural Erasure:** Historical landmarks are "decommissioned" to ensure no competing jurisdictional claim (The **Chief Cornerstone**) can be made against the new **Administrative Title**.

THE FINAL REVELATION: ARCHITECTURE AS FATE

The **Conflict Map** proves that the regional escalation is not a failure of diplomacy, but a **Success of Architecture**. The Architects did not fail to prevent the war; they successfully **designed the outcome** to facilitate a global wealth transfer.

By "knocking" on Appendix D, the Sovereign realizes that the "Impossible Hill Climb" was a scripted race. Reclaiming your agency requires you to **Step Off the Map** of the Architects and stand on the **Chief Cornerstone**.

13

APPENDIX E: THE MECHANICS OF THE SILENT EXIT

Executing the Sovereign Baseline and Asset Hardening

The shadow architecture cannot be defeated by arguing with the captured class; it is defeated by starvation. The "Silent Exit" is the physical mechanism of withdrawing your capital, your labor, and your consent from the $200B Siphon. This appendix provides the mechanical blueprint for transitioning from a "defaulting asset" on the Maritime ledger to a fully insulated Sovereign.

Phase I: The Fiat Conversion (Asset Hardening)

The Digital Guillotine (Section 4.4) relies on your wealth remaining in "Counterparty Assets"—stocks, digital bank balances, and standard retirement accounts—that can be frozen with a keystroke. True asset hardening requires the conversion of this digital illusion into physical substance.

- **The Sovereign Allocation Model:** For an individual extracting a substantial capital base—the transition requires strict ratios and absolute geographic independence. The optimal physical allocation for this tier is an approximately equal division between physical gold and physical silver.
- **Gold (The Anchor):** Provides high-density wealth preservation and protects the core baseline against the Invisible Tax of inflation.

- **Silver (The Utility):** Provides fractional utility, transactional flexibility, and high-velocity barter capability within a localized parallel economy.
- **The Vaulting Imperative:** The most critical failure point of asset hardening is storage. Bullion must *never* be held within a Tier-1 banking institution or a traditional safe deposit box, as these are subject to bank holidays, "Emergency Stability" confiscations, and digital lockouts. The asset must be secured in a private, non-systemic vault facility—entirely outside the jurisdiction of the banking cartel—fully segregated, and unencumbered by any digital tether.

Phase II: The Parallel Economy

Substance alone is not enough if you remain dependent on the system's supply chains. The Sovereign must build an analog network.

- **Localized Trust Networks:** Establish face-to-face trade relationships with local producers, tradesmen, and agricultural hubs.
- **The Barter Protocol:** Utilize your fractional silver and hard skills to bypass the Central Bank Digital Currency (CBDC) gateways entirely. When a transaction occurs outside the digital ledger, the "Strawman's Ransom" cannot be extracted.

Phase III: The Digital Phantom (De-prioritization)

You cannot immediately sever all ties without triggering the system's "Risk Profile" algorithms. The exit must be asymmetrical.

- **The Leakage Strategy:** Systematically drain fiat accounts through regular, unremarkable withdrawals rather than panicked, massive transfers that trigger Anti-Money Laundering (AML) flags.
- **The "Gray State":** Maintain the absolute minimum required digital footprint to satisfy the "Administrative Glitch" (paying the property tax, maintaining a basic utility connection) while conducting your actual life, wealth-building, and community organization exclusively on the "Land."

14

Appendix F: The Architecture of Exclusion

The Initiated, the Profane, and the Monopolization of Human Agency

This appendix details the structural and psychological mechanisms by which ruling classes—historically operating as mystery schools or secret societies, and currently operating as a modern privateer class—divide humanity to maintain a monopoly on resources, jurisdiction, and historical truth.

I. The Etymological and Structural Boundary

The division of humanity into the "initiated" and the "profane" is not a byproduct of wealth or arbitrary social prestige; it is the foundational engineering requirement for any sustained system of minority rule.

The term *profane* derives from the Latin *profanus*, literally meaning "outside the temple." In the context of systemic power, the "temple" is not a religious building, but the repository of actual chronological history, advanced physical sciences (beyond the 5% materialist spectrum), and the mechanics of administrative law.

By structurally classifying the general population as remaining outside this repository, the architects establish two distinct realms of reality:

- **The Realm of Agency (The Initiated):** Those who possess the overarching template of history and the causal mechanics of the environment.
- **The Realm of Management (The Profane):** Those who are provided a managed, linear, and strictly materialist narrative, reducing them from

sovereign actors to biological data points to be administered.

II. The Psychological Utility of Exclusion

To maintain a consolidated power structure without suffering institutional cognitive dissonance, the architects require moral insulation. The initiated/profane dichotomy provides this necessary psychological firewall.

When the uninitiated are classified as a lower order of being—analogous to the Atlantean concept of automatons or "things"—the ruling class is philosophically absolved of any moral duty toward them. One cannot commit a crime against a system resource. This internal justification is what allows for massive wealth extraction, the deployment of engineered economic resets, and endless, managed conflicts. The profane are not viewed as victims of these actions; they are viewed as the raw material fueling the machinery of the architects.

III. The Mechanics of Asymmetrical Information

Power requires an imbalance. The modern iteration of the "Sons of Belial" (Appendix A) maintains this imbalance strictly through the control of information and the suppression of chronological anomalies.

The uninitiated are educated entirely within a materialist paradigm (Scientism). They are taught that reality is limited strictly to what can be physically measured and that history is a slow, unbroken line of progress. By enforcing this limited worldview, the architects ensure the profane never develop the conceptual vocabulary required to identify cyclical catastrophism or question the legitimacy of the jurisdictional veil.

The initiated, conversely, compartmentalize the truth. Knowledge is distributed through strict degrees of initiation, ensuring that the lower echelons manage the physical administration of society while only those at the absolute apex direct the overarching, cyclical templates.

IV. Systemic Agoraphobia: The Engineered Paralysis

The restriction of conceptual vocabulary described above intentionally induces a condition of *Systemic Agoraphobia*—a psychological paralysis where the uninitiated become terrified of operating outside the synthetic boundaries of the administered system.

When the architects engineer economic volatility, societal friction, or geopolitical terror, this agoraphobia ensures the masses self-police their compliance. Because they have been denied the mechanics of natural law, they instinctively retreat deeper into the perceived safety of fiat wealth and legal fictions (*Financial Agoraphobia*) rather than stepping into the unprotected, open space of absolute sovereignty. The physical cage is therefore unnecessary; the profane are engineered to fear the exit.

V. The Modern Privateer Class

Historically, a privateer was an entity authorized by a sovereign state to conduct piracy without being bound by the legal constraints of a formal navy. The secret society model has evolved entirely into a modern privateer class.

Today, this class operates through highly centralized networks of high finance, multinational corporate governance, and technology conglomerates. They exhibit the exact hallmarks of the ancient initiated orders:

- They are heavily subsidized and protected by sovereign states, yet they operate entirely outside the boundaries of standard constitutional or administrative law.
- They consolidate global resources and direct societal outcomes with zero accountability to the "profane" public.
- They view national borders and local legal jurisdictions merely as administrative illusions—useful for managing the uninitiated, but entirely irrelevant to the architects themselves.

VI. Conclusion: The Ultimate Monopoly

The ultimate objective of dividing the initiated from the profane is not merely financial wealth or temporary political control; those are secondary symptoms. The primary objective is the total monopolization of human agency.

By hoarding the structural truths of the physical and spiritual environment and classifying the rest of humanity as uninitiated material units, the architects attempt to exclusively write the script of reality, forcing the masses to merely act out their assigned roles within a fabricated timeline.

15

Appendix G: The Scripted Apocalypse & The Permanent War Economy

The Synthesis of Mystery Babylon and the 1984 Blueprint

This appendix codifies the mechanical application of "Sacred Scripting" used by the Privateer Class to manage global transitions. It bridges the ancient jurisdictional exclusions of **Appendix F** with the modern psychological and economic warfare documented by **William Cooper** and **George Orwell**.

I. The Tactical Script: Revelation as Managed Event

The Privateer Class does not view eschatology as a series of future events to evolve naturally; they utilize the **Book of Revelation as a literal tactical manual**.

- **The "Mother of Harlots" Infrastructure:** The script utilizes the "Mystery Babylon" entity—a global, city-based religious and political system (traditionally linked to Rome/Vatican but expanded to include all "Initiated" centers)—to ride the "Beast" of global administrative power.
- **Engineered Fulfillment:** High-level initiates use the script to deliberately stage "plagues, famines, and rumors of wars" (e.g., the $200 oil threshold and the Strait of Hormuz closure). This forces a global psychological alignment with an "Apocalyptic" inevitability.

- **The Purpose of the Mirror:** By mirroring biblical narrative, the Architects strip the individual of agency, convincing the "profane" that the current engineered chaos is "Prophesied" and therefore unchangeable. This induces **Systemic Agoraphobia**—a terror of the collapsing old world so profound that the masses willingly run into the arms of a "New World Order" solution.
- **The False Return:** The final phase involves a staged "solution" to the chaos, intended to mimic a messianic arrival or a "New Age" of peace, which is actually the finalization of the global administrative cage.

II. The Permanent War Economy: The Orwellian Engine

As detailed in *1984*, the "Permanent War" (Oceania vs. Eurasia/Eastasia) is the primary mechanical tool for maintaining a pyramidal social structure and managing the "Void."

- **The Destruction of Surplus:** The primary function of perpetual war is the **continuous destruction of the products of human labor**. If the middle class ("The Middling") is allowed to accumulate wealth, leisure, and independent capital, they will inevitably turn their attention to the "High Class" and demand true sovereignty.
- **The "Suez" Equilibrium:** War is a "test of strategy and technology" used to justify the rationing of energy, food, and movement. By keeping the populace focused on the base of Maslow's hierarchy (searching for fuel, food, and basic safety), the Privateers ensure the masses never have the leisure or intelligence to question the legitimacy of the "Initiated" class.
- **Engineered Scarcity:** The $200 oil scenario is the modern **"Victory Gin"**—a tool of forced poverty designed to keep the seeker focused on survival so they cannot ascend to the peak of Truth.

III. The Universal Club: Jurisdictional Collusion

At the apex of the global hierarchy, there are no truly "sovereign" enemies. The leadership of opposing sides belongs to the same Mystery School "Club."

- **The "Enemy" Illusion:** Cooper and Orwell converge on the fact that the "Enemy of the People" (e.g., Emmanuel Goldstein) is a creation of the Party itself. This necessary "Other" justifies the surveillance state and redirects the frustration of the masses away from the Architects.
- **Dialectical Materialism:** The Privateer Class utilizes nations as pieces on a board, creating artificial polarities (Thesis vs. Antithesis/Left vs. Right) to drive humanity toward a pre-determined **Synthesis**: a single, digitized global authority. The "war" on the news is the theater used to finalize this jurisdictional merger.

IV. The Architecture of the Digital Cage

The transition from the "Old World" to the "New World Order" involves the replacement of physical sovereignty and objective reality with a **Managed Simulation**.

- **Newspeak and the Erasure of History:** The Ministry of Truth (Minitrue) ensures that the "profane" have no objective reference point. By constantly rewriting records and suppressing "chronological anomalies," the Privateers keep the populace in a **"Continuous Present."** * **The Architecture of Doublethink:** This allows the "Initiated" to hold two contradictory "truths" simultaneously, enabling them to manage a fraudulent reality with total sincerity.
- **The Mark of Necessity:** Economic chaos is used to force a migration into **Digital IDs and CBDCs**. Just as Orwell's citizens are forced into total dependence on the Party, access to the "market" becomes a privilege granted by the administrative state, conditional upon compliance with the "Script."

V. Forensic Conclusion: The Lure of Hope

Appendix G confirms that the **"Void"** is not empty; it is a meticulously managed simulation designed to monopolize human agency.

- **The Trap of Hope:** Legal maneuvers (like the Brunson Case) or promises of "Mass Arrests" are frequently utilized within the script as **"Lures"** to identify and trap those who still hold hope for a solution within the existing jurisdictional firewall.

- **Radical Decoupling:** The only exit from the script is to stop playing the assigned role. This requires the Truth Seeker to decouple their survival, wealth, and psychological stability from the managed timeline of the Privateer class.
- **The Defensive Posture:** This includes holding physical assets (gold/silver) outside the digital grid, maintaining an independent history, and refusing the psychological lure of the "Two Minutes Hate" generated by the managed media cycles.

Two Minutes Hate: A ritualized, daily period of intense emotional manipulation where the "profane" are conditioned to direct their cumulative fear, frustration, and existential rage away from the **Architects** and toward a scripted external enemy (e.g., **Emmanuel Goldstein**, or modern geopolitical "villains").

- **The Mechanical Function:** It serves as a psychological "pressure valve" to prevent the populace from recognizing their own jurisdictional exclusion. By focusing on a common object of hatred, the individuals lose their independent agency and become a unified, manageable mass.
- **Modern Application:** In the current **Privateer Script**, this is manifested through the 24-hour news cycle, "viral" social media outrage, and the polarization of the Iran/US conflict. It is designed to keep the Truth Seeker trapped in a state of emotional reactivity, preventing the **Radical Decoupling** necessary for true sovereignty.

16

APPENDIX H: THE 666 FIFTH AVENUE PROTOTYPE

The Architecture of Over-Leverage and the Privatization of Consequence

Introduction: The Evolution of the Privateer Playbook

The mechanics of the "Jurisdictional Void" observed in the 2026 Geneva negotiations were not spontaneously generated; they were perfected two decades earlier in the commercial real estate sector. To understand the current deployment of private equity envoys in matters of global statecraft, one must examine the foundational prototype: the January 2007 acquisition of 666 Fifth Avenue.

This transaction serves as the Rosetta Stone for the modern privateer class. It explicitly details the structural methodology used to acquire perception-altering assets through extreme institutional leverage, utilize manufactured distress to force a restructuring, and ultimately externalize catastrophic risk onto the public while retaining administrative control.

The 666 Fifth Avenue ledger demonstrates that operators within this class do not alter their underlying tactics when transitioning from commercial real estate to international diplomacy; they simply scale the size of the collateral. The same mechanics utilized to force institutional bondholders into accepting severe yield reductions in 2011 are now being applied to force sovereign nations into leveraged geopolitical treaties.

The acquisition and subsequent financial engineering of 666 Fifth Avenue provided the precise psychological and tactical framework that laid the groundwork for the 48-hour Geneva sabotage. By auditing this initial transaction, the architecture of the Tri-Lateral Engine is revealed not as a diplomatic strategy, but as a hostile, zero-sum financial acquisition scaled to the level of global conflict.

I. The Zero-Sum Acquisition (The Setup)

The Maximum Leverage Play

In January 2007, Kushner Companies executed the acquisition of the 41-story Midtown Manhattan office tower located at 666 Fifth Avenue. The purchase price was $1.8 billion, a figure that registered as the highest price ever recorded for a single office building in United States history at that time. However, the true architecture of the transaction lay not in the final price, but in the extreme ratio of its capitalization. The $1.8 billion acquisition was financed utilizing a staggering $1.75 billion in debt. By constructing a capital stack that relied on merely $50 million in personal equity, the purchasers established a loan-to-cost ratio exceeding 97%. This was not a traditional real estate investment; it was an exercise in maximum institutional leverage. The vast majority of the capital originated from Barclays Capital and UBS Real Estate Securities, which subsequently divided the primary $1.215 billion senior mortgage into tranches and securitized it into the Commercial Mortgage-Backed Securities (CMBS) market.

The Privateer Blueprint

This transaction establishes the foundational financial mindset and operational blueprint of the privateer class. The objective is never the slow accumulation of equity through operational cash flow or traditional stewardship. Instead, the blueprint demands the immediate securing of massive, perception-altering assets using almost entirely borrowed institutional capital. By injecting only a fractional percentage of personal equity, the privateer practically eliminates personal financial exposure while simultaneously achieving maximum jurisdictional and administrative control over the asset. The capital provided by the public—through the pension funds, insurance companies, and mutual funds that ultimately purchased the securitized debt—serves as the unacknowledged leverage. The privateer dictates the terms of the vessel, while the institutional investors assume the catastrophic risk of a market collapse. This framework allows for absolute control decoupled from proportional consequence, a mechanism that becomes infinitely more destructive when scaled from commercial property to sovereign statecraft.

II. The Manufactured Distress and the "Haircut" (The Siphon)

The Collapse of Yield

The vulnerability of the maximum leverage play materialized immediately following the acquisition, coinciding with the 2008 financial crisis. Between 2008 and 2010, the commercial real estate market contracted, office rents plummeted, and major tenants vacated the property. Consequently, the building's net operating income (NOI) experienced a catastrophic decline, rendering it incapable of covering the massive monthly debt service required by the $1.215 billion senior mortgage. By 2010, the property's valuation had plummeted from the underwritten $2 billion pro-forma to a distressed appraisal of merely $820 million. The debt service coverage ratio dropped to approximately 0.60x, meaning the asset was structurally insolvent and generating only sixty cents for every dollar owed in interest. This collapse of yield created the necessary conditions for the next phase of the operation: utilizing engineered financial distress as offensive leverage against the creditors.

Forcing the Siphon

Facing an asset appraised at hundreds of millions of dollars less than its primary mortgage, the privateers executed the 2011 restructuring. Instead of absorbing the loss and forfeiting the property to foreclosure, the threat of total default was weaponized. A fire-sale foreclosure in a depressed market would have guaranteed devastating, immediate principal losses for the institutional bondholders holding the securitized Commercial Mortgage-Backed Securities (CMBS). Operating under this duress, the special servicer representing these bondholders—who effectively managed the capital of public pension funds, insurance policies, and mutual funds (the "People Farm")—was forced to capitulate to a draconian restructuring. The $1.215 billion mortgage was bifurcated into a $1.1 billion "A-note" and a subordinate $115 million "B-note." Crucially, the interest rate on the primary debt was slashed from over 6.3% to a laddered rate beginning at a mere 3%. This drastic reduction in interest yields constituted the "haircut," a mechanism forcibly siphoning expected returns away from the public ledger to temporarily stabilize the privateer's vessel.

The Asymmetric Consequence

The 2011 restructuring cemented the operational reality of the privateer class: the absolute decoupling of control from consequence. The institutional investors and the managed public definitively absorbed the financial damage of the initial over-leveraged bet, enduring years of suppressed yields and frozen capital to keep the property afloat. In stark contrast, the privateers did not face the customary penalty of capitalist failure. By utilizing the institutional capital's own fear of catastrophic loss against it, the privateer successfully shifted the financial burden of the distressed asset onto the public while retaining full administrative and operational control of the building. The architecture of the transaction ensured that the privateer maintained their jurisdictional foothold at the exact expense of the populations whose capital had financed the original acquisition.

III. The Institutional Bailout and Erasure (The Exit)

The 99-Year Lease

By 2018, the artificially stabilized primary debt of the 2011 restructuring approached its impending maturity date. The privateers, having extracted years of administrative control without sustaining personal equity loss, faced a final reckoning as traditional refinancing remained impossible for the still-distressed asset. The exit strategy required a massive, external institutional bailout. In August 2018, Brookfield Asset Management injected approximately $1.28 billion in an upfront cash payment to acquire a 99-year ground lease on the office portion of the property. This sudden capital infusion functioned as the final rescue mechanism, allowing the complete and immediate payoff of the restructured $1.1 billion senior debt. The privateer successfully exited the catastrophic 2007 acquisition having never absorbed the principal losses that would have ruined a traditional market participant. The massive institutional apparatus of Brookfield absorbed the physical asset and the financial burden of its necessary, long-term rehabilitation.

Erasing the Ledger

The final phase of the privateer protocol is the complete sanitation of the historical record. Following the execution of the 99-year lease, Brookfield initiated a $400 million physical overhaul and executed the immediate rebranding and renumbering of the building from 666 Fifth Avenue to "660 Fifth Avenue." This administrative alteration was not merely cosmetic; it represents the privateer's inherent ability to fundamentally erase the history of financial distress, operational failure, and the deep cultural stigma attached to the original address. By changing the physical nomenclature of the asset, the historical ledger is effectively wiped clean. The narrative is permanently reset, ensuring that the legacy of the maximum leverage play and the subsequent forced institutional haircut is buried beneath a new facade. The privateer walks away unencumbered by reputational or financial ruin, free to deploy the exact same architecture of over-leverage and externalized risk against the next target.

IV. The Geopolitical Prologue (The Synthesis)

Scaling the Playbook

The historical ledger of 666 Fifth Avenue is not an isolated financial event; it is the direct operational prologue to the geopolitical maneuvers detailed in Chapter VI. The exact methodology developed in the commercial real estate sector—acquiring control of massive assets through extreme institutional leverage, utilizing manufactured distress to force counterparts into draconian negotiations, and externalizing all catastrophic risk onto the public—constitutes the precise psychological and tactical framework currently being deployed by these same actors in Middle Eastern diplomacy. When these private equity envoys orchestrated the 48-hour Geneva sabotage, they were not inventing a new diplomatic strategy; they were executing a proven real estate maneuver on a global scale. They utilized the threat of regional military conflict as the "manufactured distress" to force sovereign counterparts into leveraged agreements, all while relying on massive external capital infusions—such as the sovereign wealth funds of the Gulf Monarchies—to ultimately underwrite and bail out the geopolitical transaction.

The Ultimate Conclusion

The ultimate conclusion drawn from this forensic audit is that the privateer class does not alter its fundamental tactics when transitioning from the boardroom to the theater of global statecraft. The mechanics of the siphon remain identical. The only variable that changes is the scale and nature of the collateral. In 2007, the collateral was a single commercial property, and the externalized risk was borne by institutional bondholders and pension funds. In the current geopolitical arena, the collateral has been scaled up to encompass sovereign nations, and the externalized risk—inflationary taxation, destabilized global energy markets, and kinetic warfare—is borne by the global public. The privateer's playbook remains a static, mechanical instrument of wealth transfer and jurisdictional control, utilizing the sovereign authority of the state merely as leverage to execute the ultimate zero-sum acquisition.

17

The Bridge: Prelude to the Celestial Breach

The Final Audit: Closing the Material Ledger

You have just completed a forensic examination of the *Consolidation of the Void*. Through these pages, we have tracked the movement of capital from the "People Farm" into the privateer accounts of the Affinity Partners. We have identified the specific hardware of the $5 Billion Parallel and the administrative erasure of the State Department.

However, the Truth Seeker must realize that the financial theft was merely the "Ground Floor." The extraction of wealth was the *distraction*; the extraction of **The Living Soul** is the objective. The "Void" described in Volume I is not a vacuum—it is a prepared frequency fence, a clearing of the jurisdictional deck intended to facilitate a transition from **Economic Slavery** to **Neural Enclosure.**

The Shift: From Hardware to Frequency

If *Consolidation of the Void* was about the **Hardware** of the system, *The Celestial Breach* is about the **Transmission**.

The privateer class has realized that material control is incomplete without the "Neural Hijack." They have initiated a "Breach" into the very high-ground of human consciousness, historical legacy, and atmospheric reality. The tactics you have learned—Reflexive Dismissal and the Scapegoat Protocol—are now being broadcast through a **Synthetic Epiphany** designed to overwrite your innate discernment.

Volume II: The Advanced Briefing

In the forthcoming volume, *The Celestial Breach*, we move the audit into the deep-spectrum vectors of the adversary's new tactic:

- **The Frequency Lexicon:** Why reclaiming your own grammar is the only way to avoid the "Joinder" of the managed state.
- **The Atmospheric Siege:** An analysis of **V2K (Voice to Skull)**, Neural Hi-jacks, and the Ionization of the air we breathe as a method of jurisdictional foreclosure on the body.
- **The Cosmic Machinery:** Deconstructing the **Lunar Governor** and the **Satellite Trap** to reveal the proximity illusions that maintain the "Closed Roof" of our current reality.
- **The Genetic Patent:** How the adversary seeks a "Divine Patent" through biological compliance, and the **Yehoshua Protocol** required to execute a total jurisdictional mutiny.

The Sovereignty Uplink

As you move into the next phase of this trilogy, the **Reference Note** must be applied to your own biology. It is no longer enough to audit the bank; you must now audit the air, the light, and the frequency.

1. **The Jurisdiction:** Recognize that the "Void" is being filled with the **Noahide Protocol**—a universal administrative framework designed to catch the "uninitiated."
2. **The Adversary's Tactic:** Look for the **Synthetic Epiphany**. Be wary of "Uplinks" and "Downloads" that do not originate from the Chief

Cornerstone.

3. **The Response:** Move from "Functional Decoupling" to a **Jurisdictional Mutiny**. The Heir does not negotiate with the Privateer; the Heir reclaims the Estate.

The Final Proclamation

The mirage is breaking, but the "Conductor" is calling. The **Celestial Breach** is your manual for navigating the **Stockholm Architecture** of the digital cage. This is the roadmap for those who refuse to be "biological data points" and instead choose the path from **Jacob to Israel**.

18

Conclusion

The Anatomy of the Snare and the Sovereign Response

The trajectory of modern economic history and geopolitical maneuvering points toward a singular, orchestrated destination: the consolidation of all power, wealth, and autonomy into a centralized void. The impending implementation of Central Bank Digital Currencies (CBDCs) is not a natural evolution of finance, but the final mechanism of a digital panopticon. It is the ultimate snare, designed to strip the individual of the very concept of personal and spiritual sovereignty.

The Nature of the Trap The architecture of this control grid relies on absolute dependency. A programmable currency allows the pillars of deception to dictate, monitor, and restrict every transaction, movement, and choice. When access to the economic system is contingent upon compliance with shifting mandates, the illusion of freedom evaporates. From an eschatological perspective, this represents a definitive threshold. The system demands that individuals trade their sovereignty for the convenience and necessity of participation, funneling humanity into a void where independent thought and action are systematically neutralized.

Identifying the Adversary's Tactic The greatest weapon wielded by the architects of this system is unawareness. The snare is set by gradually normalizing surveillance, centralizing resources, and masking mechanisms of control as societal safety or technological progress. To succumb to this normalization is to forfeit sovereignty willingly. The truth seeker must look at the geopolitical landscape without the filter of mainstream narratives and recognize the CBDC infrastructure for exactly what it is: a tool of absolute, undeniable subjugation.

The Action Required Awareness alone is insufficient without corresponding action. Maintaining sovereignty requires a deliberate, daily walk outside the boundaries of this impending grid. This involves:

- **Divestment from the Pillars of Deception:** Actively minimizing reliance on the centralized medical, banking, and entertainment industries that serve as the foundation of the control grid.
- **Building Parallel Systems:** Cultivating localized independence, securing tangible assets, and establishing networks that operate outside the digital panopticon.
- **Anchoring in the Truth:** Refusing to compromise spiritual sovereignty for physical comfort. The sovereign mind must remain rigorous in its analysis, testing every new global mandate against the established facts of this consolidation effort.

The void only consumes those who march into it blindly. For the truth seeker who identifies the problem, the path forward is clear. It requires vigilance, a rejection of the systems designed to ensnare, and an unwavering commitment to the truth at all costs.

Afterword: The Responsibility of the Truth Seeker

To engage in a rigorous analysis of geopolitics, economic history, and eschatology is to accept a distinct burden. The architecture of the void—the interlocking systems of financial control, medical mandates, and media deception—relies on the passive acceptance of the masses. Once the mechanics of this digital panopticon are clearly identified, they cannot be unseen. The illusion of benign global progress shatters, leaving only the uncompromising reality of the snare.

The framework presented in *The Consolidation of the Void* is not designed to be passively consumed; it is a blueprint for continuous application. The adversary's tactics will evolve. The terminology surrounding programmable currencies, global health security, and centralized governance will shift to appear more palatable to the undiscerning mind. The responsibility of the truth seeker is to apply the analytical rigor established in these pages to every future mandate and geopolitical realignment.

Sovereignty is not secured by a single realization. It is maintained through a daily, deliberate walk. It requires the constant testing of new information against established historical and theological facts. It demands the discipline to recognize when the pillars of deception are attempting to encroach upon personal and spiritual territory, and the fortitude to refuse compliance.

You now possess the anatomy of their system. The task before you is to utilize this understanding not as a source of fear, but as a tactical advantage. Let the facts dictate your preparations, guard your sovereign mind with unyielding vigilance, and demand the truth at all costs.

Epilogue

The Enduring Remnant

The architecture of the void is vast, funded by the consolidated wealth of nations, and enforced by a digital apparatus designed to measure and mandate every human action. To observe the final assembly of this system—the programmable currencies, the centralized health directives, the relentless geopolitical realignments—is to witness the culmination of an ancient blueprint. The snare is set, and the majority will walk into it, trading the heavy burden of freedom for the sterile convenience of compliance.

Yet, the fundamental weakness of this control grid is that it requires consent. It is a system built entirely on the illusion that physical and economic survival are the highest forms of existence.

For the truth seeker, the analysis does not end in despair; it ends in clarity. The ultimate objective of this global consolidation is not merely the management of resources, but the capture of the human spirit. To recognize this is to neutralize their primary weapon. When the mind is sovereign, the parameters of the digital panopticon lose their absolute authority. The physical constraints may tighten, but the spiritual territory remains entirely out of their reach.

The path forward requires a conscious, daily separation from the pillars of their deception. It demands the discipline to operate parallel to a collapsing system rather than integrating with it. History and eschatology both confirm that consolidated power ultimately fractures under its own weight. The void is not infinite; it is temporary.

Until that fracture occurs, the mandate for the sovereign individual is unwavering. Stand apart. Hold fast to the facts. Maintain an uncompromising grip on the truth. The truest victory over the void is simply refusing to let it consume you, ensuring that when the final accounting is made, you are found standing as a good and faithful servant to the truth.

A Look Ahead: The Trilogy Continues

The analysis of the control grid is only the beginning. The timeline continues in the upcoming volumes of the trilogy.

The Celestial Breach As the void solidifies its economic and geopolitical hold, the focus shifts to the eschatological timeline unfolding above and around us. This second volume explores the spiritual and celestial ramifications of a subjugated humanity, detailing the specific historical shifts that follow the establishment of the digital panopticon and the fracturing of established narratives.

Well Done, Good and Faithful Servant The final volume addresses the ultimate fate of the sovereign mind. It provides the definitive conclusion to the eschatological analysis, offering a rigorous blueprint for the remnant to maintain their spiritual sovereignty and stand uncompromised when the final accounting is made.

About the Author

About the Author

Robert- John: [Kauffmann] is an independent researcher, author, and truth seeker whose work focuses on the forensic deconstruction of systemic deception. After a decades-long career operating within the traditional financial and professional frameworks of the modern era, he executed a "Functional Exit" to pursue a disciplined, fact-based analysis of the global power structures he identifies as the **Architecture of Deception**.

His approach is rooted in the belief that truth must be able to withstand the rigors of any analytical scrutiny. As the architect of *The Sovereignty Trilogy*, he synthesizes complex geopolitical data, metaphysical history, and administrative law into a tactical briefing for those navigating the "Jurisdictional Void." His work serves as a navigational guide for the **Remnant**, emphasizing the restoration of individual standing through the **Yehoshua Protocol** and the rejection of the **Biometric Tether**.

Following the completion of the inaugural volume, *Consolidation of the Void*, his research has transitioned into the deep-spectrum audit found in *The Celestial Breach* and the final jurisdictional proclamation of *Well Done Good and Faithful Servant*. His commitment to maintaining a distinction between the biological **Living Man** and the corporate **Strawman** is reflected not only in his writing but in his personal administrative protocols and daily walk.

Now residing in Steamboat Springs, Colorado, he balances the intensive demands of his "Sovereignty" research with the grounded, analog reality of seasonal work as a carpenter's helper. This integration of high-level theological study and physical craftsmanship allows him to maintain a unique vantage point—operating "in the world, but not of it." Whether priming and painting a drywall repair, managing a sourdough fermentation, or auditing a $200 billion legislative siphon, he remains dedicated to the pursuit of the **Chief Cornerstone** and the reclamation of human agency.